PAINTED FABRIC FUN
Simple and Stylish Projects for Your Home

Jennifer R. Ferguson and Judith A. Skinner

Martingale®
& COMPANY

CREDITS

President ■ Nancy J. Martin

CEO ■ Daniel J. Martin

Publisher ■ Jane Hamada

Editorial Director ■ Mary V. Green

Managing Editor ■ Tina Cook

Technical Editor ■ Dawn Anderson

Copy Editor ■ Liz McGehee

Design Director ■ Stan Green

Illustrator ■ Laurel Strand

Cover and Text Designer ■ Shelly Garrison

Photographer ■ Brent Kane

Painted Fabric Fun:
Simple and Stylish Projects for Your Home
© 2005 by Jennifer R. Ferguson
and Judith A. Skinner

Martingale & Company
20205 144th Avenue NE
Woodinville, WA 98072-8478 USA
www.martingale-pub.com

Printed in China
10 09 08 07 06 05   8 7 6 5 4 3 2 1

Library of Congress Cataloging-in-Publication data is available upon request.

ISBN 1-56477-577-1

Mission Statement

Dedicated to providing quality products
and service to inspire creativity.

Dedication

From Jennifer

To my loving husband, Jim. Without your continued support, none of my projects would ever come to light. I don't even know if words could ever express the love I have for you; you are not only the one I share life with, but also my very best friend that I can share anything and everything with. You are always there to pick up where I fall short, always there for our children, and always there to keep me laughing when I'm truly ready to cry. I owe so much to you; thanks for sharing all this with me. I love you.

From Judy

To my daughter, Corri. I love my boys but always wanted a little girl. Watching her grow from a little girl to a grown woman with a daughter of her own has been one of the great joys of my life. When you have this little girl, you don't realize she will grow up to be your best friend. We share our thoughts and feelings and talk to each other once a day. I love you and thank you for being you. Love, Mom

Acknowledgments

Jennifer would like to thank her kids, Ashley and Tyler, for again putting up with the process of another book and for hanging in there with smiles.

Judy would like to thank her family: her husband, Don; their children and family members, Donnie, Josh, Presli, Rex, Joanie, Corri, Bob, and Samantha; and her brother Richard for all the odd jobs or what she refers to as "jopy" jobs. Without all their help, none of this would have been possible.

Jennifer and Judy would like to thank the following people for their contributions to this book:

The owners of Quilters' Paradise in Clovis, California: Colette, Barbara, and Kathy. Thank you all for your guidance and help with the quilt projects. They never would have been accomplished without your assistance.

Cynthia McGunigle and Liana Brigham for doing an incredible job on the custom quilting for both of the quilts.

Sandy Findley of the Dawn Co., Inc., for all the work you did on the window shade and covered cornice; neither project would have been completed without you.

Shann Zimmerman Tavares of Terry's Upholstery. Once again, you have outdone yourself with the incredible job on the upholstered projects.

The staff at Martingale & Company. Your continued support over the years has just been unbelievable. You are all always there to answer questions and take care of everything.

Mary Green of Martingale & Company. Jennifer would like to extend a personal thank-you for your guidance and assistance on this project.

Brent Kane. Once again you truly amaze us with your talent behind that lens. We missed being there during photography, but nothing was missed in your photos.

Most important, we would like to thank all of the readers who have bought our books over the years. You have made all this possible. We hope that we have assisted you with your projects, inspired you to create more, and put a smile on your face.

Finally, a personal thank-you from Jennifer to her staff: Trudy, Penny, Cindy, and Cheryl. You have all kept my store running and projects going, and given me the support I needed so that this book could be completed. Many thanks to all of you for your help and friendship.

CONTENTS

When painting is your passion, it's hard to leave any surface untouched. Over the years, Jennifer dabbled in fabric painting, doing a little here and there, and then realized that she wasn't dabbling at all—in fact, she's taught many classes on fabric painting and has painted quite a few of the fabrics in her own home.

As you look around your home, you'll notice all the opportunities that exist for you to paint on fabric. Fabrics offer a way to add color and pattern to a room. You can also stencil seasonal projects to decorate for the holidays or just to change things from season to season. If you are new to the art of stenciling, fabric provides a wonderful surface to begin on, and once you get going on the fabric projects, you'll want to do more. You might even want to stencil some coordinating walls or furniture projects—the possibilities are endless.

We chose many of the project surfaces based on how easy they were to find locally or by mail. Some you may already own. It's amazing how much a little paint and a stencil design can change the appearance of an everyday item. It is easy to create sheets and pillowcases to match the decor of a room, to customize draperies and window shades, or to make a covered cornice. We found many projects to paint, and we hope

that our creativity will inspire you to try your hand at fabric painting.

Getting started is easy; *Painted Fabric Fun* will guide you through every step of the process. First, you'll learn about tools and supplies and how to select fabrics suitable for painting. Then, we will teach you how to prepare your project and fabric for painting. Next, you'll explore the world of decorative painting; we have explained each technique in detail. Finally, you'll learn how to personalize your decorated project and protect its painted surfaces. We've even included a section on quilting basics for those interested in making a quilt with painted quilt bolcks. Once you've browsed through these sections of *Painted Fabric Fun*, you'll be ready to choose a project and begin. We hope, of course, that your first project inspires you to create many more.

Every one of the projects featured in this book comes with step-by-step instructions that will guide you from start to finish. To help beginning painters achieve professional results, we've named the specific colors that we used to paint each project, and we've also explained which colors are used with each stencil. Of course, you may want to combine techniques and designs from several different projects to create a uniquely decorated painted-fabric project of your own.

TOOLS AND SUPPLIES

In this section, we discuss the tools and supplies we used to prepare and paint the projects in this book. Our first list, "General Tools and Supplies," covers standard items and products. These are the items you'll want to have on hand no matter which project you choose to work on. Our second list, "Technique-Specific Tools and Supplies," covers items that are required for certain projects.

General supplies

GENERAL TOOLS AND SUPPLIES

Shop for the items on this list at your local home-improvement store, at craft- and art-supply stores, or by mail order (see "Suppliers" on page 95). You may already have some of these items around the house.

AC's Acrylic Craft Paint Remover and a Sanding Sponge

Use a sanding sponge (medium, 100 grit) and AC's Acrylic Craft Paint Remover to remove dried acrylic paint from stencils (available through the Stencilled Garden; see "Suppliers" on page 95).

Acrylic Paints

Acrylic craft paints come in a wide range of colors, are easy to apply, and dry quickly. We used DecoArt Americana acrylics to paint several of the projects in this book (see the individual project instructions for the specific colors). You'll need one two-ounce bottle of each color unless noted otherwise. Please note that acrylic colors dry darker than they appear in their bottles. To test a color, brush some of the paint onto a piece of scrap fabric and let it dry.

Artist's Brushes and Stencil Brushes

Build your own assortment of flat, round, and angle-tipped artist's brushes from ¼" to 1½" wide. Artist's brushes yield smoother finishes than ordinary paintbrushes. They are perfect for applying sealers, primers, and base coats. They are also used in some decorative-painting techniques. For stenciling, you'll need stencil brushes. For a closer look at brushes, see "Choosing Brushes" on page 9.

Artist's Water Basin

An artist's water basin serves as both a brush holder and a rinsing basin for your artist's brushes.

Brush Cleaner/Conditioner and Brush Scrubber

Use a brush cleaner/conditioner and a brush scrubber to clean stencil brushes. A cleaner/conditioner is better for your brushes than soap alone. Brush scrubbers are small plastic implements with thin teeth that you use to help remove the paint from stencil-brush bristles.

Cardboard or Foam-Core Board

You'll need smooth-finish cardboard or foam-core board for your fabric-painting surface. Spraying the board with a repositionable spray adhesive and smoothing your fabric onto it will keep the fabric in place and prevent the fabric from pulling or stretching while you are painting. Cut the cardboard or foam-core board to a size that is appropriate for the project you are working on.

Cotton Swabs

Cotton swabs work well for fixing small painting mistakes. While the paint is still wet, moisten a swab and use it to wipe away any unwanted paint. Swabs can also support wooden ball knobs as you paint them and as the paint dries on them (see "Base-Coat Painting" on page 15).

Drop Cloth or Newspaper

Before you begin a project, protect your work surface with a drop cloth or several layers of newspaper.

Extender

Acrylic paint extender is a liquid that is mixed into acrylic paints to increase the amount of time that the paints stay wet. Adding a drop or two of extender to each color you use will make the paint more manageable and help create smooth painted effects. Extender is especially useful when stenciling. It comes in two-ounce bottles.

Fabric-Painting Medium

This medium, which comes in two-ounce bottles, converts acrylic paints into fabric paints. It softens and improves adhesion of acrylic paints to textiles. Mix two parts paint to one part medium.

Fabric Paints

We have used DecoArt SoSoft Fabric Acrylics for most of the projects in this book. SoSoft Fabric Acrylics are supersoft, brush-on fabric paints that are opaque, give excellent coverage, and are highly durable on washable fabrics. SoSoft Fabric Acrylics are soft like fabric dye but don't require heat-setting and are permanent.

Paint Palette

You'll never dip a brush directly into a bottle of paint. Instead, you'll squeeze some paint onto a palette and load your brush from it. A pad of disposable artist's palettes makes for easy cleanup. Just tear off the used sheet when you're done painting and throw it away. Disposable plastic plates make good substitutes.

Paint Pen

For signing your finished masterpiece, a fine-tipped black paint pen is convenient and easy to handle.

Painter's Tape

Use removable painter's tape (also known as "blue tape") to affix stencils to your projects. When you peel off the tape, you won't remove your freshly painted finish along with it.

Paper Towels

Use folded paper towels to remove excess paint from stencil brushes. This paint-removal process is known as "off-loading." You'll also need paper towels for your wet bags (see "Wet Bags" on page 9).

Precut Stencils

A precut stencil is a plastic sheet with a pattern of holes (or windows) cut out of it. Design motifs are added to a project by applying paint through the window openings. We used precut Stencilled Garden stencils to create the projects in this book (see "Suppliers" on page 95). The project instructions list the specific stencil designs and paint colors we used. Of course, you can substitute other stencil designs and paint colors if you want. Stencils are usually packaged in plastic bags. Save the bags; they'll help protect your stencils when you're not using them.

Repositionable Spray Adhesive

Spray adhesive is applied to the smooth side of a piece of cardboard or foam-core board to create a sticky surface to secure fabric for painting. It helps the fabric lie flat and prevents the fabric from shifting during the stenciling process.

Scissors

Keep a pair of good scissors on hand for cutting fabric and use craft scissors for cutting sandpaper.

Wet Bags

For stenciling, you must start out with stencil brushes that are completely dry. You'll need one brush for each paint color. As you switch back and forth between brushes, you'll place the paint-loaded brushes that you're not using into a "wet bag" so the paint on them won't dry out before you need to use them again. To make a wet bag, moisten a paper towel, squeeze out the excess water, fold the towel, and place it in an open plastic bag. Store your paint-dampened stencil brushes in the wet bag, with their bristles resting on the damp paper towel, until you are ready to use them again.

CHOOSING BRUSHES

Your painting will always be at its best if you choose the right brush for the job. Here are descriptions of the artist's and stencil brushes we used to create the projects in this book.

Angular

The bristles of these flat brushes are trimmed at an angle. They're great for applying colors in tight corners and for painting one color next to another.

Flats

Flat brushes, with their squared-off bristles, are ideal for priming, base-coat painting, blocking in large areas of color, and varnishing.

Long Liners

Also called script-liner brushes, these brushes have very long bristles that come to a sharp point. These brushes are your best choice for painting fine lines.

Stencil Brushes

You'll need several stencil brushes, ranging from ¼" to 1" in width. Unlike artist's brushes, stencil brushes are round and have stiff bristles and blunt ends.

TECHNIQUE-SPECIFIC TOOLS AND SUPPLIES

To find out which of these items you'll need, just refer to the "Tools and Supplies" list that accompanies the project you've selected.

Technique-specific tools and supplies

Acrylic Polymer Varnish

This varnish dries to a durable flexible finish, which is what's needed for a floorcloth. If a stiff varnish is used, the varnish can crack on this flexible surface.

Basic Woodworking Tools

Keep a hammer, some pliers, screwdrivers, a palm-held sander, and a tape measure on hand. You'll use these tools for repairing, sanding, and other prepping and finishing tasks.

Batting and Foam

You'll need one or both of these for some of the projects, such as the upholstered rocker and covered cornice. You'll also need batting for the quilt and wall hanging.

Bowling-Alley Paste Wax

This wax is used over the varnished floorcloths. It protects the surface and gives an easy cleanup finish (available from Home Trends; see "Suppliers" on page 95).

Chip Brushes

Inexpensive chip brushes have rough, stiff bristles, which are wonderful for applying glazes.

Cotton Rags

This type of rag makes a wonderful texture in glazes. You'll use this type of rag to "pounce" out the glaze finish on the pull-down window shade on page 50.

Decorative Accents

This catchall category includes rope cording, fringe, tassels, trims, wooden dowels, and drawer pulls. These items are used in several of the projects in this book.

E6000 Industrial-Strength Adhesive

Use this adhesive to attach wooden ball knobs to projects. Be sure to follow the manufacturer's instructions.

Embossing Tool

This crafter's tool is a stick with a small, hard metal ball at one or both ends. The balls are usually used to emboss paper, but you'll use them to create "La De Da Dots" (see "La De Da Dots" on page 18).

Faux-Glazing Medium

This pigment-free medium increases translucency. You'll mix this medium with acrylic paint to create a glaze mixture. It was used on the pull-down window shade on page 50.

Floorcloth Canvas

This is a heavyweight canvas (10- to 12-ounce cotton duck) that comes pre-primed on both sides. It has a stiff feel and makes a great surface for painted floorcloths.

Foam Block or Egg Carton

A rigid foam block (used in floral crafts) or an egg carton becomes a handy drying stand for freshly painted wooden ball knobs (see "Base-Coat Painting" on page 15).

Foam Roller

Use a foam roller to apply a solid area of paint to a large surface such as a floorcloth.

Friendly Woodworker or Advanced Woodworking Tools

A few of our projects require advanced woodworking skills and tools, such as jigsaws and table saws. You may want to do what we did and recruit a local woodworker to tackle these parts of the project for you.

Gesso

Gesso is a very thick, water-based artist's primer that yields an opaque, smooth finish. You'll need this special primer for the stenciling technique called "whiting out" (see "To white out" on page 17).

Goggles

To protect your eyes from fine dust particles, wear goggles whenever you are sanding.

Hot Glue Gun and Glue Sticks

You'll need these to attach cording and fringe to several of the projects.

Iron and Ironing Board

You may need to press your fabrics before painting them. An iron and ironing board are necessary for pressing seams and hems on sewing projects such as the stenciled quilts. You'll also need an iron to heat-set projects painted with a mix of acrylic paints and fabric-painting medium.

Plywood

Some projects require additional wood components. We used ¼"-thick plywood to make the pieces we needed.

Press Cloth

Use a press cloth to cover your painted design when you are heat-setting acrylic paint that has been mixed with fabric-painting medium. We use a piece of cotton or organza. See "Heat-Setting" on page 14.

Primer

You should prime a wood surface before painting it. We use water-based primer, since our acrylic paints are also water-based. A primer coat acts to seal the wood and creates an excellent foundation for subsequent layers of paint to adhere to.

Respirator or Dust Mask

Whenever you are sanding wood, wear a respirator or dust mask and work in a well-ventilated area, preferably outdoors. Inhaling the airborne particles created during sanding isn't good for your health.

Rubber Pad or Rug Gripper

This pad is cut slightly smaller than a floorcloth and placed underneath it so the rug will stay in place and not slip.

Sandpaper

Purchase sheets of sandpaper in several different grits or degrees of roughness: coarse (40 to 60 grit), medium (80 to 120 grit), and fine (150 to 220 grit). You'll need the sandpaper to prepare wood surfaces before you paint them and to smooth dried coats of paint.

Sewing Supplies

A few of the projects in this book require the use of a sewing machine and general sewing supplies. If you are making a project such as a quilt, wall hanging, or slipcover, you may need the following: sewing machine, rotary cutter, transparent graph ruler, self-healing cutting mat, sewing-machine needles, hand-sewing needles, pins, sewing shears, and fabric marking pens.

Staple Gun and Staples

Use a staple gun to secure fabric to wood surfaces, such as was done on the covered cornice on page 46.

Transparent Graph Ruler

You'll use a 2"-wide, 18"-long graph ruler and watercolor pencil to mark off areas for painted borders and stripes. Because you can see through them, these rulers are especially useful when you're trying to align one marked line with another.

Transparent Medium

Transparent fabric medium mixed with acrylic paints and fabric paints creates a translucent wash for fabrics.

Varnishes

Protect finished wood projects with several coats of water-based varnish. Use an interior varnish for projects that will remain indoors. Use an exterior varnish for projects that you plan to set outdoors.

Watercolor Pencils or Fabric Marking Pens

Watercolor pencils or fabric marking pens are ideal for marking stripes and for marking off borders. Use light-colored pencils and pens so the lines won't show through the paint that covers them.

Wood Putty

Use wood putty to fill any cracks, dents, or holes in your project before painting it.

Wood Screws

Use wood screws to join two pieces of wood together and also to attach the wooden ball knobs to one of the projects. Wood screws come in different lengths and diameters; you'll need to choose a size that's appropriate for your project. Glue is sometimes used in addition to screws for an extra-strong join.

Wood Sealer

Apply a water-based wood sealer to unfinished wood to prevent warping. Apply several coats of sealer to any knots in the wood. This will prevent pitch from bleeding out of the knots and through the primer and finishes you apply.

Wooden Ball Knobs

A wooden ball knob is a round ball with one flat surface and a hole running partway into its center. We attach these knobs to several projects to serve as bun feet. They come in several different sizes.

THE FABRIC

When purchasing an item to paint on, or fabric that will be painted and then sewn into an item, choose a fabric that has the texture or lack of texture that you desire for your project.

Paint can react differently on different types of fabric. The smoother the finish of the fabric, the smoother the painting will be. A more textured fabric, such as a woven natural denim, will have plenty of texture in the painting.

Natural-fiber fabrics tend to work best, especially for an item that will receive regular washing. If choosing a synthetic fabric, make sure you are creating a project that will need very little, if any, washing.

Also, when looking for fabrics, don't limit yourself to solid colors. Sometimes it is fun to start with a printed fabric and stencil additional designs over the patterns. This creates an interesting layered look.

SURFACE PREPARATION

Before you paint your project, whether it is fabric or another surface, you must prepare the surface, or the paint you apply won't adhere properly.

PREPARING FABRIC

Before painting on any fabric item, prewash it, making sure to follow the washing instructions provided by the manufacturer. This process is necessary to remove all starch, marks, and impurities in the fabric. Use soap, but don't add fabric softeners. If purchasing fabric yardage, take into account that most fabrics will shrink, so buy at least 10% more than needed.

It's nice to line-dry the fabric, if possible, or you can use a machine dryer. Remove the fabric or fabric items from the line or dryer before completely dry and iron the fabric smooth.

PREPARING AN OLD WOOD SURFACE

Sanding will usually remove loose particles of the existing paint finish and roughen up the surface of the project. This roughening up is important because new paint won't adhere to a slick finished surface. Start with a medium- to coarse-grit sandpaper and change to a finer-grit sandpaper as the work progresses. Remember to wear goggles and a respirator or dust mask. If possible, do your sanding outdoors; you'll be generating a lot of dust. When you're finished sanding, wipe the project with a tack cloth or lint-free rag to remove any dust.

If your project is rickety, repair it or have a woodworker repair it for you. Use wood putty to fill any holes, pits, or dents that are marring the project surface. Allow the putty to dry, following the manufacturer's instructions, and then sand the area lightly to make the putty filler level with the surrounding wood.

The next step is priming. Use a water-based primer and a flat artist's brush, 1" to 1½" wide. Apply several thin, even coats of primer to the entire project. For the smoothest possible finish, keep your brush strokes going in the same direction. After the primer has dried, sand it lightly with your finest-grit sandpaper and then wipe away the sanding dust with a tack cloth or lint-free rag.

PREPARING A NEW WOOD SURFACE

You won't always be working with old wood; you may find it more convenient to start with a new wood piece instead of recycling something old.

Sand the surface with medium- to fine-grit sandpaper. Work outdoors if you can, and remember to wear goggles and a dust mask or respirator. Always sand the piece in the same direction as the wood grain. If the wood surface has dents, cracks, or nail holes in it, fill them with wood putty, allow the putty to dry, and sand it smooth. Wipe the project with a tack cloth or lint-free rag when you're finished.

The next step is sealing. Use a wood sealer and a flat artist's brush, 1" to 1½" wide. Apply a thin, even coat of wood sealer to the entire project surface. The sealer will help prevent warping and will also raise the wood grain slightly. Allow the sealer to dry; then sand the surface with fine-grit sandpaper and wipe with a tack cloth or lint-free rag. If the wood has any knots, seal them several times more, drying and sanding lightly between applications. Sealing the knots will help prevent pitch from bleeding out of knots and through the painted finish.

After sealing comes priming. Follow the same priming method as for an old wood surface described at left.

There are many different paint products available for painting on fabric. We have used two different paint mediums in this book: DecoArts Americana Acrylic paints and SoSoft Fabric Acrylics. For projects that combine both painted fabric and painted wood, we have used DecoArts Americana Acrylic paints for the wood surfaces.

For painting on fabric, our first choice is always a fabric paint. Even though sometimes these product lines have a limited range of colors, we prefer the fabric paints because they stay soft and have great washability. Having the paints remain soft can be a priority, depending on the project you are working on. For example, sheets and pillowcases need to stay very soft, so the choice for this project was SoSoft Fabric paints.

Our second choice is the wide range of wonderful colors that are available with the Americana acrylics. When using this paint on fabric, mix one part fabric-painting medium to two parts paint to soften the acrylics and give them great adhesion to the fabric. This paint dries a little stiffer than fabric paint so we needed to take that into account when selecting which projects to use it on. You'll also need to heat-set fabric painted with Americana acrylics after the paint has dried completely.

With so many paint choices, you may want to experiment with several different paint types and brands on some sample fabric. This will give you an idea of the texture you'll be creating and is also a wonderful way to test colors on the fabric before you start painting on your project.

HEAT-SETTING

To heat-set acrylic paint, first allow the paint to dry for 24 to 48 hours. Cover the painted area with a press cloth; then, with your iron set to the appropriate fabric setting, apply heat to the painted area for at least 30 seconds. Lift iron (and press cloth as necessary), move to the next section, and repeat. Continue until the entire painted area has been heat-set.

FABRIC-PAINTING SURFACE

One of the most frustrating things Jennifer dealt with when she started to paint on fabric was the pulling and stretching of the fabric. After trying several ways of dealing with the problem, she discovered a wonderful way to keep fabric stable as she worked. To create a painting surface, you'll need either a large piece of smooth cardboard or a piece of foam-core board and a repositionable spray adhesive. Spray the entire surface of the cardboard or foam-core board with the adhesive and allow it to set up for a minute or two; then smooth your fabric over this surface. The spray adhesive holds the fabric, keeping it from stretching as you paint. If the adhesive starts to loosen its hold, just apply another layer to the cardboard or foam-core board.

BASE-COAT PAINTING

Once you've finished preparing the surface of your project, you'll be ready to paint the base coat. The base coat is the foundation for all the decorative painting that follows.

Read the individual project instructions to learn which base-coat colors to use on your project and where to apply them. Pour a little paint onto a paint palette and work some of it into a flat artist's brush. Brush the paint onto the project, always stroking in the same direction. If the paint won't brush on smoothly, dip your brush into water to moisten it slightly before working the paint into the bristles.

Allow the first coat of paint to dry. If the painted surface is rough, use your finest-grit sandpaper to smooth it, but be careful to remove as little paint as possible. Wipe away any dust with a tack cloth or lint-free rag. Apply as many coats of paint as necessary to achieve smooth, opaque coverage, letting each coat dry before applying the next.

To paint a wooden ball knob, insert one end of a cotton swab into the hole in the knob. Use the other end of the swab as a handle so that you don't have to touch the knob itself. When you finish sealing, priming, or painting the knob, insert the free end of the swab into a foam block to hold the knob upright for drying. You can also prop the knob and its swab handle in an empty egg carton for drying.

DECORATIVE PAINTING

This section provides complete instructions for all the decorative painting techniques featured in this book. You don't need to memorize every detail; just turn back to these pages whenever you need to refresh your memory.

STENCILING

Stenciling is a remarkably easy painting technique. If you've never tried it before, we suggest practicing on paper before tackling your project.

We used stencils from the Stencilled Garden for all of our projects. These stencils are available at specialty stencil shops and from mail-order suppliers (see "Suppliers" on page 95). Each set of project instructions specifies which stencils to use and which paint colors to apply. Of course, you may also choose to substitute other stencil designs.

To position the stencil: Place your stencil on the project, locating the open design cutouts over the areas where you'd like the painted designs to appear; then tape the outer edges of the stencil to the project with removable painter's tape.

To load and off-load the stencil brush: Pour a little paint onto a paint palette, add one or two drops of extender, and use the handle end of your stencil brush to mix in the extender well. Next, holding your stencil brush straight up, pick up a small amount of paint with the tips of the brush bristles. Work the paint into the bristles by swirling them in a circular motion on a clean section of the palette.

One trick to successful stenciling is to have only the tiniest amount of paint on your brush bristles, which is referred to as a "dry brush." To off-load the excess paint, hold the brush upright and with a firm, circular motion, rub the bristles on a folded paper towel. Then, on a clean portion of the paper towel, wipe the brush in an X motion to remove excess paint from the outer bristles.

To apply the paint: For a smooth stenciled surface, "swirling" is the best technique to use. Hold your stencil brush perpendicular to the project surface and apply the paint by moving the bristle ends in tiny circles. To add texture and depth to a stenciled design, hold the brush perpendicular to the surface, but instead of swirling the bristles, dab the brush straight up and down, a process known as "stippling."

To create shading in the stenciled design, first create sharp, crisp edges by applying paint lightly all the way around the outer edges of the design opening. As you work, blend paint into the interior-design area but apply less pressure to the brush. You'll notice that the color appears lighter toward the center of the design. By varying the pressure you apply to your brush and the amount of time you spend stenciling a given area, you can achieve a wide range of values with a single color.

For added contrast within a design, use more than one color. Let each color dry before applying the next, use a different brush for each color, and leave the stencil in place until you've applied all the colors. (Once you've removed a stencil, it's very difficult to realign it in exactly the same position.)

To white out: Before stenciling on top of a black or dark-colored base coat, you must "white out" the areas where your stenciled designs will appear. Otherwise, your stenciled colors won't show up well.

Whiting out is easy. Position your stencil on the project and secure it with tape. Use a stencil brush to apply gesso through the stencil. Leave the stencil in place and allow the gesso to dry. (If you like, you may use a blow dryer to speed up the drying process.) Then stencil your design with the desired colors directly over the white gesso coat. Never remove the stencil until you've applied all the colors.

To clean and store stencils and brushes: After using a stencil, you should clean it as soon as possible. The longer the paint remains on the stencil, the harder it will be to remove. Unfortunately, cleaning is hard on stencils and it is all too easy to damage them.

One way to clean stencils is with AC's Acrylic Craft Paint Remover, available from the Stencilled Garden (see "Suppliers" on page 95). Place the stencil in a sink. Pour the cleaner over it, let everything sit for a minute or two, and then gently scrub off the paint with a fine-grit sanding sponge. Rinse the stencil with warm water to remove the cleaner.

Another way to clean stencils is to use hot water and a bit of elbow grease. Place the stencil under hot running water and rub it gently with the sanding sponge.

To dry a stencil after cleaning it, place it on a towel and either let it air-dry or pat it dry with a paper towel. Store clean stencils in their original plastic bags, stacking the bags so that the stencils lie flat.

To clean a stencil brush, first moisten the bristles under running water and scrub them over the surface of a brush scrubber. Next, apply brush cleaner/conditioner to the bristles and scrub them over the brush scrubber again. Rinse the bristles under water. Repeat until the suds are clear and colorless. Squeeze out the excess water and place the brush on its side to dry.

COLOR WASHING

A color wash is a mixture of paint and transparent medium. It is applied to the fabric surface to create a faded, uneven look. We have used color washing in a variety of ways, including creating a washed background to stencil on, adding a wash of color around a stenciled design, and creating stripes and borders with a color-wash mixture. To make the wash for borders or stripes, mix as much as four parts transparent medium to one part acrylic paint or fabric paint. To create a color wash for backgrounds and washing around stenciled motifs, mix eight parts transparent medium to one part acrylic paint or fabric paint.

Brush the wash onto the fabric with a stencil brush. Use a scrubbing, back-and-forth motion, keeping all the strokes going in the same direction. If you're new to this technique, practice on a piece of scrap fabric with the same wash mixture you plan to use on your project. First, affix your fabric onto your painting surface (cardboard or foam-core board sprayed with repositionable spray adhesive). Then mix and apply the wash mixture to the fabric. To darken a wash mixture, just add more paint (acrylic or fabric) to the mixture; to lighten a wash mixture or make it more transparent, just add more of the transparent medium to the mixture.

NEGATIVE GLAZED FINISHES

Negative glazed finishes are applied over a base coat to create aged textures and colors. Start by pouring four parts faux glazing medium into a mixing tub. Add one part paint and mix with a stirring stick.

Use a chip brush to apply the glaze mixture to your project. To create the textured finish and also to eliminate brushstrokes, wad up a terry-cloth rag and "pounce" it over the glazed surface, removing the excess glaze. Allow the finish to dry thoroughly. If the first application of glaze isn't dark enough to suit you, apply more glaze coats as desired, allowing each coat to dry before applying the next.

Negative glaze finish with stenciling

STRIPES AND BORDERS

To make stripes or borders, start by measuring and marking off the stripes or borders with a transparent graph ruler and a light-colored watercolor pencil or fabric marking pen (a). Then cut pieces of removable tape and position them just along the outer edges of each marked line (b). Using your finger or the side of a brush handle, press down and burnish the edges of the tape to help prevent paint from seeping under them.

To create a color-wash mixture for stripes and borders, mix four parts transparent medium with one part acrylic or fabric paint. (This diluted mixture will yield a soft-colored stripe or border.) Then, with a stencil brush, apply the paint mixture to the area between the two pieces of tape or the bordered area (c). Remove the tape after painting the stripes and borders (d).

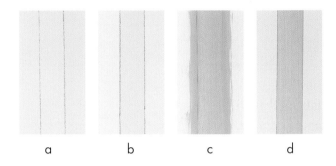

a   b   c   d

LA DE DA DOTS

La De Da Dots are simply raised dots of paint. Pour a little paint onto your palette. To make the dots, touch one end of an embossing tool to the paint, picking up a small amount, and then touch the tool to the project to transfer the color and create a raised dot. Repeat this process for every dot. The secret to dots that are raised and not flat is to pick up fresh paint from the palette for each dot that you make.

Beginners sometimes have trouble spacing their dots, bunching them up in some areas and scattering them too far apart in others. To prevent this problem, visualize a small triangle in the middle of the area to be painted. Apply a dot to each point of the imaginary triangle. Now visualize another triangle linked to the first one. Apply dots to the points of this second triangle. If you continue applying dots in this way, you'll find that they are evenly spaced.

We've always found it fun to personalize our projects by signing and dating each piece. When Judy's grandson, Josh, was very young and tried to say "Judy", out would come "Jubee" instead. Judy began signing her work this way, writing the letters "Ju" followed by a stenciled bee. Jennifer signs each piece differently. If the piece is a gift to someone, she often writes a personal message for the recipient. At other times, she just signs "J. Ferguson" and the date.

The last step is to apply varnish to wood pieces and floorcloths, and Scotchgard to all fabrics that will be handled, such as chairs, stools, and ottomans. Varnish and Scotchgard are very important, because they protect all the work you've put into your masterpiece. For wood, use

a water-based varnish and apply it with a flat artist's brush. To avoid drips and runs, apply at least two or three thin, even coats. Allow each coat to dry thoroughly before applying the next. For our stenciled fabrics, we use spray-on Scotchgard. Read the manufacturer's instructions for applying the product to your stenciled fabric.

QUILTING BASICS

Jennifer admits that she is not a quilter, or at least not yet, but it is on her to-do list. The quilts in this book were assembled and quilted by professionals with the help of the wonderful people at Quilters' Paradise. Following are some general quilting instructions that will help you with the two quilt projects in this book. Additional quilting resources that you might find useful are *Your First Quilt Book (or it should be!)* by Carol Doak and *The Magic of Quiltmaking* by Margaret Rolfe and Jenny Bowker. Both books are published by Martingale & Company.

GENERAL GUIDELINES

The fabrics used on these projects were all light-weight 100% cotton, 44" wide. Sew all seams with a ¼"-wide seam allowance. It is important

to maintain exact ¼"-wide seam allowances; otherwise, the quilt blocks will not be the desired finished size. This will affect how well they fit together and also how well the sashings and borders fit together. If you have a machine foot that measures exactly ¼" from the center needle position to the edge of the foot, you can use the edge of the presser foot as a guide; otherwise, create a seam guide by placing a piece of tape on the machine ¼" from the needle. After stitching, press the seam allowances to one side, toward the darker fabric, unless otherwise directed.

MARKING THE QUILTING LINES

It is not necessary to mark all quilting lines. If you plan to stitch in the ditch of the seam line, outline quilt a uniform distance around the stenciled designs, or free-motion quilt in a random pattern, you won't need to mark quilting lines. However, for more complex designs, mark the quilt top before layering it with batting and backing. A variety of marking tools are available for marking your quilting lines. Use a sharp No. 2 pencil on light-colored fabrics and a yellow or silver marking pencil on dark fabrics. Or you can use a chalk pencil to mark your lines. Test the marking tool first on a scrap of fabric to be sure the marks remove easily.

LAYERING THE QUILT

To prepare for quilting, make a quilt "sandwich" by layering the backing, batting, and quilt top. Cut the backing and batting about 4" larger than the quilt top all around. For large quilts, you'll need to piece two or three lengths of fabric together to make a backing the required size. Press the backing seams open to make quilting easier. Batting comes packaged in standard bed sizes, or it can be purchased by the yard. Select a thin batting if you intend to quilt by hand or machine.

To layer the quilt:

1. Spread the backing, wrong side up, on a flat, clean surface. Anchor it with pins or masking tape, being careful not to stretch the fabric out of shape.

2. Place the batting over the backing and smooth out any wrinkles.

3. Place the quilt top, right side up, over the batting and smooth out any wrinkles. Be sure the edges of the quilt top are parallel to the edges of the backing.

4. If you plan to quilt the layers by hand, baste the layers with a needle and thread as follows: Start in the center and work diagonally to each corner.

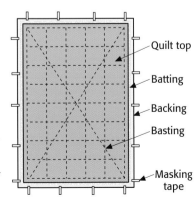

Quilt top

Batting

Backing

Basting

Masking tape

Continue basting in a grid of horizontal and vertical lines 6" to 8" apart. Finish by basting around the edges.

If you plan to quilt the layers by machine, baste the layers with No. 2 rustproof safety pins, placing the pins 6" to 8" apart, away from the area you intend to quilt.

QUILTING

Both of the quilts in this book were machine quilted by professional quilters in a free-motion style to enhance the stenciled artwork. You may choose to do the quilting yourself.

For free-motion quilting, you'll need a darning foot and the ability to drop or cover the feed dogs on your sewing machine. With free-motion quilting, you don't turn the fabric under the needle, but instead guide the fabric in the direction of the design. This technique requires some practice. Practice on some scrap fabric until you feel comfortable with the design you have chosen. For additional information on machine quilting, refer to *Machine Quilting Made Easy!* by Maurine Noble (Martingale & Company, 1994).

BINDING

For a French double-fold binding, cut binding strips 2½" wide across the width of the fabric. You'll need enough strips to go around the perimeter of the quilt, plus 10" for seams and the corners in a mitered fold.

1. Sew strips, right sides together, to make one long piece of binding. Join strips at right angles and stitch across the corner as shown. Trim the excess fabric and press the seams open.

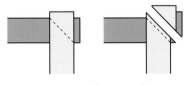

Joining Straight-Cut Strips

2 Fold the strip in half lengthwise, wrong sides together, and press. Turn under ¼" at a 45° angle at one end of the strip and press.

Fold line

3 Trim the batting and backing even with the quilt top. If you plan to add a sleeve (at right) for hanging, do so now before attaching the binding.

4 Starting on one side of the quilt and using a ¼"-wide seam allowance, stitch the binding to the quilt, keeping the raw edges even with the quilt-top edge. End the stitching ¼" from the corner of the quilt and backstitch. Then clip the thread.

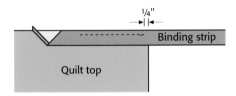

¼"

Binding strip

Quilt top

5 Turn the quilt so that you'll be stitching down the next side. Fold the binding up, away from the quilt, and then back down onto itself, parallel with the edge of the quilt top. Begin stitching at the edge, backstitching to secure. Repeat on the remaining edges and corners of the quilt.

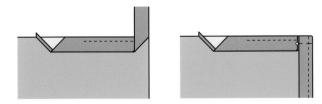

6 When you reach the beginning of the binding, overlap the beginning stitches by about 1" and cut away any excess binding, trimming the end at a 45° angle. Tuck the end of the binding into the fold and finish the seam.

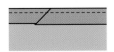

7 Fold the binding over the raw edges of the quilt to the back, with the folded edge covering the row of machine stitching, and blindstitch in place. A miter will form at each corner. Blindstitch the mitered corners.

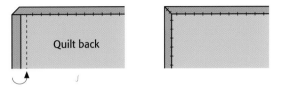

Quilt back

ADDING A SLEEVE FOR HANGING

To display your quilt on a wall, add a fabric sleeve to the back of the quilt to hold the rod.

1 Using leftover fabric from the front or a piece of muslin, cut a strip 6" to 8" wide and 1" shorter than the width of the quilt at the top edge. Fold the short ends under ½" and then ½" again, and stitch close to the first fold.

2 Fold the fabric strip in half lengthwise, wrong sides together, and baste the raw edges to the top edge of the quilt back. The top edge of the sleeve will be secured when the binding is sewn to the quilt.

Baste sleeve to top edge of quilt.

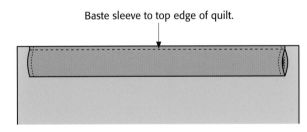

3 After the binding has been attached, insert the hanging rod into the sleeve and pin the sleeve along the lower edge. Remove the rod and blindstitch along the lower edge of the sleeve.

GIRLY GIRL'S WHIMSY QUILT
QUEEN QUILT

This quilt was designed and created for Jennifer's daughter, Ashley. They spent a wonderful afternoon at Quilters' Paradise picking out the fabrics, and Ashley's participation in the project truly helped make this a one-of-a-kind family heirloom.

Finished Quilt Size: 90" x 113½"

TOOLS AND SUPPLIES

Yardages are based on 42"-wide fabric.

- 3⅛ yards of off-white 200-thread-count cotton for painted blocks (fabric A)

- 1⅞ yards of blue print for outer border (fabric B2)

- 1 yard of yellow print for middle border (fabric B8)

- ½ yard of black print for inner border (fabric C)

- ¼ yard *each* of 12 different fabrics for sashing strips (fabrics B1–B12)

- 8½ yards of fabric for backing

- 1 yard of green print for binding (fabric B3)

- 98" x 122" piece of batting

- Thread to match fabrics

- Iron and ironing board

- Sewing supplies

- Acrylic paints and stencils (see page 23)

- General tools and supplies (pages 7–9)

PAINTS AND STENCILS

We used the following paints and stencils to create our "Girly Girl's Whimsy Quilt" (see "Suppliers" on page 95). For a different look, substitute the colors or stencils of your choice.

DecoArt SoSoft Fabric Acrylics

- Deep Periwinkle Blue (DSS56)
- Primary Blue (DSS42)
- Hauser Light Green (DSS47)
- Hauser Dark Green (DSS46)
- Lamp Black (DSS24)

Stencilled Garden Stencils

- Girly's Flower Border (TSG122)

CUTTING

Prepare the off-white 200-thread-count cotton fabric for painting (see "Preparing Fabric" on page 13). Cut all fabric strips across the width of the fabric.

From fabric A, cut:
12 squares, each 18" x 18"

From *each* of fabrics B1–B12, cut:
4 strips, 3½" x 18"
4 squares, 3½" x 3½"

From fabric C, cut:
9 strips, 1½" x 42"

From fabric B8, cut:
9 strips, 3½" x 42"

From fabric B2, cut:
10 strips, 6" x 42"

From fabric B3, cut:
10 strips, 2½" x 42"

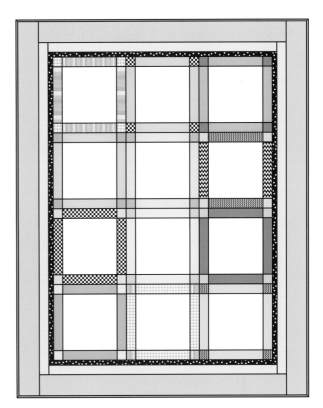

Quilt Plan

☐ Fabric A	▨ Fabric C	
▦ Fabric B1	☐ Fabric B5	■ Fabric B9
☐ Fabric B2	▧ Fabric B6	▨ Fabric B10
▨ Fabric B3	▨ Fabric B7	▨ Fabric B11
☐ Fabric B4	☐ Fabric B8	☐ Fabric B12

STENCILING

1. Smooth out one of the fabric A squares onto the cardboard painting surface (see "Fabric-Painting Surface" on page 14).

2. Stencil the designs, referring to the project photo as necessary. For detailed stenciling instructions, see "Stenciling" on page 15. Repeat for each of the cotton fabric squares. Set aside and allow to dry.

ASSEMBLING THE QUILT

1. Sew together a stenciled fabric square, four matching sashing strips, and four matching squares to make a stenciled block as shown. Refer to the quilt plan on page 23 for placement of the fabrics.

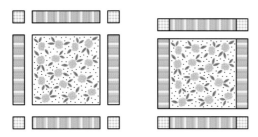

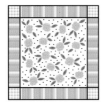

Stenciled Block
Make 12.

2. Arrange the blocks into four rows of three blocks each, using the quilt plan as a guide. Sew the blocks into horizontal rows and press the seam allowances to one side as indicated

by the arrows, alternating the pressing direction from row to row as shown. Join the rows together.

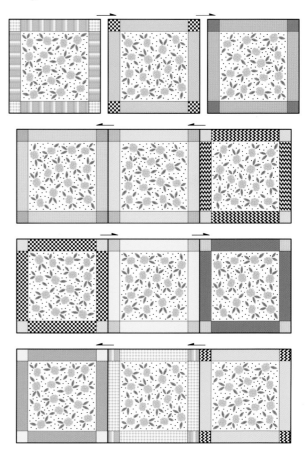

3. Measure the width of the quilt top through the center. Cut fabric C strips to this measurement, piecing as necessary. Mark the center of the quilt edges and border strips. Pin the borders to the top and bottom edges

of the quilt top, matching the center marks and ends, and easing as necessary. Sew the border strips in place. Press the seam allowances toward the borders.

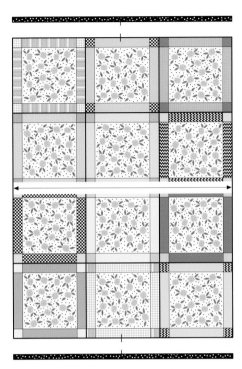

Measure center of quilt,
side to side. Mark centers.

④ Measure the length of the quilt top through the center, including the top and bottom borders just added. Cut fabric C strips to this measurement, piecing as necessary. Mark the center of the quilt edges and the border strips. Pin the borders to the side edges of

the quilt top, matching the center marks and ends and easing as necessary; stitch. Press the seam allowances toward the borders.

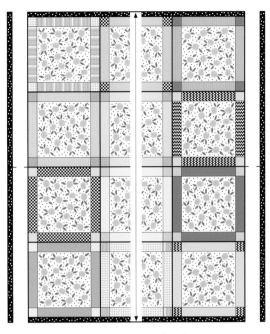

Measure center of quilt,
top to bottom, including borders.
Mark centers.

⑤ Referring to steps 3 and 4, measure, trim, and sew the fabric B8 strips to the quilt top in the same manner as for the fabric C strips. Repeat for the fabric B2 strips.

⑥ Referring to "Quilting Basics" on page 19, layer the quilt top with batting and backing. Quilt as desired and then bind the edges of the quilt.

⑦ Sign and date your quilt. If you have named the quilt, also add the name under your signature.

ALL PIECED TOGETHER
QUILTED WALL HANGING

Jennifer's inspiration for this wall hanging was a billiard room that has a two-story wall. The wall probably could have been left bare, but Jennifer felt it needed something. Working with all the colors and patterns in the room, she painted individual pieces of fabric with different designs and joined them to other coordinating fabric pieces to make a wall hanging. This approach worked well with the eclectic look of the room.

Finished Quilt Size: 43½" x 49½"

TOOLS AND SUPPLIES
Yardages are based on 42"-wide fabric.

- ¾ yard of beige print (fabric A)
- ⅞ yard of dark red-and-cream check for piecing and outer border (fabric H)
- ⅝ yard of printed text fabric if cut on the lengthwise grain, or ¼ yard if cut on the crosswise grain (fabric B)
- ⅜ yard of off-white fabric (fabric C)
- ¼ yard of yellow print (fabric D)
- ¼ yard of black fabric for inner border (fabric I)
- ⅛ yard of red print (fabric E)
- ⅛ yard of black polka dot (fabric F)
- ⅛ yard of black-and-white check (fabric G)
- 3 yards of fabric for backing
- ⅜ yard of black polka-dot fabric for binding (fabric J)
- 52" x 58" piece of batting
- Thread to match fabrics
- Iron and ironing board
- Sewing supplies
- Acrylic paints and stencils (see page 27)
- General tools and supplies (pages 7–9)

PAINTS AND STENCILS

We used the following paints and stencils to create our "All Pieced Together" project (see "Suppliers" on page 95). For a different look, substitute the colors or stencils of your choice.

DecoArt SoSoft Fabric Acrylics

- Christmas Red (DSS25)
- Alizarin Crimson (DSS55)
- Avocado Green (DSS19)
- Antique Gold (DSS2)
- Dark Chocolate (DSS23)
- Lamp Black (DSS24)
- Hauser Light Green (DSS47)

Stencilled Garden Stencils

- Fresco Grapes (TSG409S)
- Bella Flourish Border (TSG530L)
- Italian Grape Trellis (TSG531S)
- Fancy Flourish (TSG538L)
- Bacchus Diamond (TSG539L)
- Villa Francisco Scroll (TSG527)
- Dimensional Classic (TSG148)
- Girly's Scatter Pattern (TSG123)

STENCIL COLOR GUIDE

Fresco Grapes: Christmas Red, Alizarin Crimson, Avocado Green

Bella Flourish Border: Alizarin Crimson, Antique Gold

Italian Grape Trellis: Dark Chocolate, Lamp Black

Fancy Flourish: Christmas Red, Alizarin Crimson

Bacchus Diamond: Lamp Black

Villa Francisco Scroll: Antique Gold, Avocado Green, Alizarin Crimson

Dimensional Classic: Primary Red, Alizarin Crimson, Lamp Black

Girly's Scatter Pattern: Primary Red, Alizarin Crimson, Hauser Light Green, Avocado Green

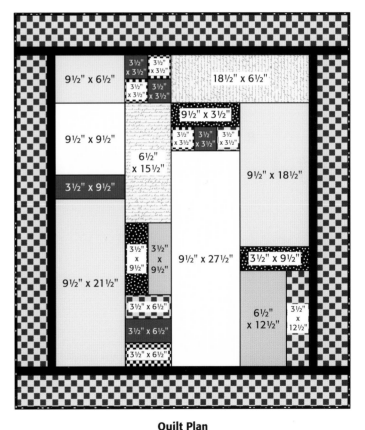

Quilt Plan

Fabric A	Fabric C	Fabric F	Fabric I
Fabric B	Fabric D	Fabric G	Fabric J
	Fabric E	Fabric H	

Cutting

Prepare fabrics A, B, C, and D for painting (see "Preparing Fabric" on page 13). Cut all fabric strips across the width of the fabric. (Cut fabric B strips on the lengthwise grain of the fabric if desired.)

From fabric A, cut:
1 piece, 9½" x 21½"
1 piece, 6½" x 9½"
1 piece, 9½" x 18½"

From fabric B, cut:
1 piece, 6½" x 15½"
1 piece, 6½" x 18½"

From fabric C, cut:
1 square, 9½" x 9½"
1 piece, 9½" x 27½"

From fabric D, cut:
1 piece, 6½" x 12½"
1 piece, 3½" x 9½"

From fabric E, cut:
1 piece, 3½" x 9½"
1 piece, 3½" x 6½"
3 squares, 3½" x 3½"

From fabric F, cut:
3 pieces, 3½" x 9½"

From fabric G, cut:
1 piece, 3½" x 6½"
3 squares, 3½" x 3½"

From fabric H, cut:
1 piece, 3½" x 12½"
1 piece, 3½" x 6½"
1 square, 3½" x 3½"
5 strips, 4½" x 42"

From fabric I, cut:
5 strips, 1½" x 42"

From fabric J, cut:
5 strips, 2½" x 42"

Stenciling

1. Referring to the project photo and the quilt plan on page 27, select one of the eight pieces of fabric to be stenciled. You will stencil the fabric A, B, and C pieces, and the 6½" x 12½" piece of fabric D. Smooth out the fabric piece onto the cardboard painting surface (see "Fabric-Painting Surface" on page 14).

2. Stencil the designs, referring to the project photo as necessary and to the "Stencil Color Guide" provided on page 27. For detailed stenciling instructions, see "Stenciling" on page 15.

3. Repeat steps 1 and 2 for the remaining seven pieces of fabric to be stenciled. Allow the paint to dry.

Assembling the Quilt

1. Refer to the project photo and the quilt plan on page 27 for placement when assembling the quilt top. Sew together the 6½" x 9½" piece of stenciled fabric A, the 9½" x 9½" piece of stenciled fabric C, the 9½" x 21½" piece of stenciled fabric A, and the 3½" x 9½" fabric E piece as shown to make section 1 of the quilt top.

Section 1

2 Stitch together two 3½" fabric E squares and two 3½" fabric G squares as shown to make a Four Patch block.

3 Stitch together a 3½" x 9½" piece each of fabrics F and D along one long edge to make unit F/D.

4 Sew together the Four Patch block, the 6½" x 15½" piece of stenciled fabric B, unit F/D, and a 3½" x 6½" piece each of fabrics H, E, and G as shown to make section 2 of the quilt top.

Section 2

5 Stitch together one 3½" square each of fabrics G, E, and H, in that order, to make unit G/E/H. Then sew together a 3½" x 9½" piece of fabric F, unit G/E/H, and the 9½" x 27½" piece of stenciled fabric C as shown to make unit 1. Stitch together the

3½" x 12½" piece of fabric H and the 6½" x 12½" piece of stenciled fabric D to make unit H/D. Stitch together a 9½" x 18½" piece of stenciled fabric A, a 3½" x 9½" piece of fabric F, and unit H/D as shown to make unit 2.

Unit 1   Unit 2

6 Join units 1 and 2 lengthwise and then stitch the 6½" x 18½" piece of stenciled fabric B to the upper edge of units 1 and 2 as shown to make section 3.

Section 3

7 Referring to the project photo and to the quilt plan on page 27, join sections 1, 2, and 3 of the quilt top.

8 Measure the length of the quilt top through the center. Cut inner and outer border strips to this measurement. Join the inner and outer border strips together in pairs. Mark the center of the quilt edges and the border strips. Pin the borders to the sides of the quilt top, matching the center marks and ends and easing as necessary. Sew the border strips in place. Press the seams toward the borders.

Measure center of quilt, top to bottom.
Mark centers.

9 Measure the width of the quilt top through the center, including the side borders just added. Cut inner and outer border strips to this measurement, piecing as necessary. Join the inner and outer border strips together in pairs. Mark the center of the quilt edges and the border strips. Pin the borders to the top

and bottom edges of the quilt top, matching the center marks and ends and easing as necessary; stitch. Press the seams toward the borders.

Measure center of quilt, side to side, including borders.
Mark centers.

10 Referring to "Quilting Basics" on page 19, layer the quilt top with batting and backing. Quilt as desired and then bind the edges of the quilt.

11 Sign and date your quilt. If you have named the quilt, also add the name under your signature.

SIMPLY SOPHISTICATED CHECKS AND SWIRLS
ROCKING CHAIR

No matter where Jennifer goes, it seems that every trip turns into a junking trip, or at least, she seizes every opportunity to look for treasures. While attending a painting convention in Houston, Texas, she found an old rocker, and it reminded her so much of "Cherries Jubilee" from *Painted Chairs*, the first book that she and Judy wrote, that she had to have it. Fortunately, she knew someone who was driving from Houston back to Fresno; otherwise, the chair might never have made it to California. Jennifer painted the fabric for this chair and had an upholsterer recover the cushions for her. To make your own ruffled box cushion, see page 32.

TOOLS AND SUPPLIES

Determine fabric and trim yardages by measuring the existing chair cushions and adding a little extra. For ruffle yardage on the seat cushion, refer to "Making Your Own Ruffled Box Cushion," step 2 on page 32.

- Old rocking chair frame
- Heavy natural-colored denim fabric for seat and back
- Rope welting for trim
- Acrylic paints and stencils (see below)
- General tools and supplies (pages 7–9)

PAINTS AND STENCILS

We used the following paints and stencils to create our "Simply Sophisticated Checks and Swirls" chair (see "Suppliers" on page 95). For a different look, substitute the colors or stencils of your choice.

DecoArt Americana Acrylic Paints
- Lamp Black (DA67)
- Glorious Gold (DA71)

DecoArt SoSoft Fabric Acrylics
- Lamp Black (DSS24)
- Glorious Gold—Metallic (DSM19)

Stencilled Garden Stencils
- Gingham (TSG112L)
- Sinclair Swirls (TSG535)

STENCIL COLOR GUIDE
Gingham: Lamp Black Fabric Acrylic

Sinclair Swirls: Metallic Glorious Gold

INSTRUCTIONS

1. Prepare the chair for painting (see "Preparing an Old Wood Surface" on page 13).

2. Using the Lamp Black acrylic paint, apply as many base coats as necessary to achieve smooth, opaque coverage on the entire chair (see "Base-Coat Painting" on page 15).

3. Using the Glorious Gold acrylic paint, paint several small sections of the front spindles with the gold for accent. Refer to the project photo as necessary for placement of the gold paint.

4. Sign your chair and allow the paint to dry for several days. (Complete the following steps while you wait.) Then protect your painted rocker by applying at least three coats of varnish (see "Final Touches" on page 19).

5. Prepare your new fabric for painting (see "Preparing Fabric" on page 13).

6. Using the Gingham stencil (eliminate one of the overlays to create wavy checks with this stencil), stencil an allover pattern of checks on all of the fabric. Refer to the project photo as necessary and to the "Stencil

Color Guide" provided at left. For detailed stenciling instructions, see "Stenciling" on page 15.

7. Using the Sinclair Swirls stencil, randomly stencil swirls over the painted checks in an allover pattern.

8. Take the painted chair and your stenciled fabric to an upholstery shop. The upholsterer can make a new seat and back, and cover them with your fabric.

MAKING YOUR OWN RUFFLED BOX CUSHION

If you don't need to upholster the back of your chair, you can make a removable box cushion for the seat yourself. Foam in various thicknesses is available at many fabric stores and can be cut to size for you. Wrapping the foam with a layer of batting makes the foam less rigid and gives a smooth appearance to the seat.

1. Measure the length and width of the chair seat and draft a square or rectangle on kraft paper to these dimensions. Add ½" all around for seam allowances.

2. Have a piece of polyurethane foam 3" to 4" thick cut to the size of your chair seat, using the pattern from step 1 as a guide but omitting the seam allowances. From your painted fabric, cut two cushion pieces for the top and bottom of the cushion, using the pattern from step 1. Also cut a boxing strip with a width equal to the thickness of your foam, plus 1" for seam allowances, and a length equal to the perimeter of the foam plus 1" for seam allowances (piece the fabric as necessary). To add a 3" ruffled skirt to the bottom of your seat cushion, cut a 7"-wide strip of stenciled fabric equal to twice the length of one side of the chair cushion plus 1" for seam allowances. Repeat to cut ruffle strips for the remaining three sides of the cushion.

3 Fold the boxing strip in half and stitch the short ends together, using a ½" seam allowance. Press the seam open. Stitch the rope welting to the long sides of the boxing strip, using a zipper foot. Turn the ends into the seam allowance where they meet.

4 Pin mark the boxing strip into quarters on each long edge and pin mark the top and bottom cushion pieces at the center of each side. Pin the boxing strip right sides together to the top cushion piece, matching pin marks and placing the seam at the sides or back of the cushion piece to avoid a seam at the front. Stitch the pieces together along the edge of the rope welting, just inside the previous stitching, using a zipper foot. Clip into the seam allowance on the boxing strip at the corners and clip into the heading of the welting strip as necessary.

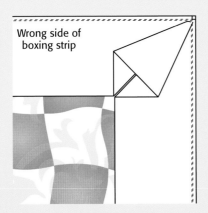

5 If adding a ruffled skirt to the seat cushion, fold each skirt length in half lengthwise right sides together and stitch along the short edges. Trim the seam allowances, turn right side out, and press ends. Pin the long raw edges together and stitch two rows of gathering stitches within the seam allowance. Pull up the gathering threads and distribute the gathers evenly. Add cushion ties if desired (see "Adding Cushion Ties" at right). Pin the

skirt pieces to the sides of the bottom cushion piece right sides together between the seam allowances and baste in place.

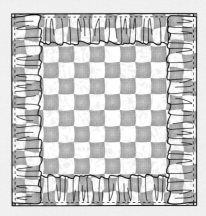

Baste ruffle pieces to each side
of the bottom cushion piece.

ADDING CUSHION TIES

If you want to add ties for securing the cushion to the chair, cut four 16" lengths of grosgrain ribbon and stitch them into the seam allowance (one on each side of the slits in the skirt) at the back of the cushion. When the seat cushion is placed on the chair, the ribbon ties should be under the skirt. Tie them around the back legs of the chair.

6 Pin the bottom cushion piece to the boxing strip, matching pin marks. Stitch as before, keeping the ruffled skirt pieces and cushion ties (if added) away from the seam allowances and leaving one side open for turning. Turn the seat cover right side out.

7 Cut a piece of batting to the dimensions of the top and bottom of the foam cushion. Also cut a strip of batting equal to the depth of the foam cushion and long enough to wrap around the perimeter of the cushion. Cover the foam cushion with the batting pieces and hand stitch the edges of the batting together. Insert the batting-covered foam cushion inside the seat cover. Slip-stitch the opening closed.

Jennifer and her daughter, Ashley, went on a trip to the Bay Area and came across an Ikea store—they don't have one locally—so they had to go shopping! They had a great day together and found this wonderful slipcovered chair that would go great in the playroom. Jennifer had been hunting for something but hadn't liked any of the fabrics that she'd seen. This slipcovered chair is wonderful, since she can remove the slipcovers for washing and can create new slipcovers if needed. This one is painted for Ashley, and Jennifer still owes her son, Tyler, a chair.

TOOLS AND SUPPLIES

- Jennylund chair (Ikea #300-475-48)
- Jennylund slipcover (Ikea #100-475-49)
- 3 bottles of transparent medium (DecoArt DSF1)
- Acrylic paints and stencils (see below)
- General tools and supplies (pages 7–9)

PAINTS AND STENCILS

We used the following paints and stencils to create our "Sunshine and Rosies" project (see "Suppliers" on page 95). For a different look, substitute the colors or stencils of your choice.

DecoArt SoSoft Fabric Acrylics

- Deep Periwinkle Blue (DSS56)
- Hauser Light Green (DSS47)
- Hauser Dark Green (DSS46)
- Antique Gold (DSS2)

Stencilled Garden Stencils

- Rosie Posie Flower (TSG200S)

INSTRUCTIONS

1. Prepare the slipcover for painting (see "Preparing Fabric" on page 13).

2. Smooth out one section of the slipcover at a time onto the cardboard painting surface (see "Fabric-Painting Surface" on page 14).

3. Randomly stencil the design onto the slipcover. Refer to the project photo as necessary. For detailed stenciling instructions, see "Stenciling" on page 15.

4. After your stenciling has dried, you'll create a washed effect all around the stenciled flowers. Mix eight parts transparent medium with one part Antique Gold paint. Using a stencil brush, scrub this wash into the fabric around all the stenciled designs (see "Color Washing" on page 17).

5. Allow the paint to dry for several days. Then sign your painted slipcover and install it onto the chair.

ALOHA TIME
SKIRTED CHAIR COVER

This wonderful "shorty" skirted chair cover was fun and easy to make and was the perfect solution for Jennifer's

home office. Jennifer found this simple chair cover perfect for hiding the flaws in her office chair.

TOOLS AND SUPPLIES

- 1 skirted slipcover for a dining chair in natural cotton duck
- Transparent graph ruler
- Transparent medium (DecoArt DSF1)
- Acrylic paints and stencils (see below)
- General tools and supplies (pages 7–9)

PAINTS AND STENCILS

We used the following paints and stencils to create our "Aloha Time" chair cover (see "Suppliers" on page 95). For a different look, substitute the colors or stencils of your choice.

DecoArt SoSoft Fabric Acrylics
- Plum (DSS53)
- Dark Burgundy (DSS50)
- Antique Gold (DSS2)

Stencilled Garden Stencils
- Hibiscus Border (TSG833)

INSTRUCTIONS

1 Prepare the skirted chair cover for painting (see "Preparing Fabric" on page 13).

2 Smooth out the skirted chair cover one section at a time onto the cardboard painting surface (see "Fabric-Painting Surface" on page 14).

3 Randomly stencil the design onto the seat and back of the chair cover. Refer to the project photo as necessary. For detailed stenciling instructions, see "Stenciling" on page 15.

4 Smooth out the skirted area of the chair cover on your painting surface. Then, using your transparent graph ruler and fabric pen, mark off approximately 1½"-wide vertical stripes on the front and sides of the skirted area (see "Stripes and Borders" on page 18).

5 Tape off all the marked stripes with removable painter's tape. Mix four parts transparent medium with one part Plum fabric paint. Using a stencil brush, scrub this wash mixture into the fabric between the taped areas, creating the stripes. Carefully remove the tape after the stripes are painted—the paint stays wet on the nonporous surface.

6 If your chair cover has ties, repeat step 5 for the ties. Create stripes on both sides of the ties.

7 Allow the paint to dry for several days; then sign and date your chair cover.

8 Place the chair cover over a dining chair.

DAISIES AND DIAMONDS
DIRECTOR'S CHAIR CANVAS

Director's chairs are comfortable both indoors and outdoors. With removable backs and seats, you can create many

different looks. Paint a set of covers for the different seasons or create a personalized chair for somebody special.

TOOLS AND SUPPLIES

- Director's chair
- Replacement canvas in natural color
- Acrylic paints and stencils (see below)
- General tools and supplies (pages 7–9)

PAINTS AND STENCILS

We used the following paints and stencils to create our "Daisies and Diamonds" project (see "Suppliers" on page 95). For a different look, substitute the colors or stencils of your choice.

DecoArt SoSoft Fabric Acrylics

- Light Soft Sage (DSS49)
- Plum (DSS53)
- Dark Burgundy (DSS50)
- Lamp Black (DSS24)

Stencilled Garden Stencils

- Double Checks (TSG713-2)
- La De Da Flowers (TSG171)

STENCIL COLOR GUIDE

Double Checks: Light Soft Sage

La De Da Flowers: Plum, Dark Burgundy

Dots: Lamp Black

INSTRUCTIONS

1. Prepare the chair canvas for painting (see "Preparing Fabric" on page 13).

2. Smooth out the chair canvas, one piece at a time, onto the cardboard painting surface (see "Fabric-Painting Surface" on page 14).

3. First, stencil the check pattern, positioning the stencil so the checks are on point to create a diamond pattern. Stencil the diamond pattern as an allover repeat on both pieces of the canvas. Then, stencil the flowers randomly on top of the diamonds, grouping two or three flowers together if desired. Finally, stencil the "dot" at each diamond intersection that was not covered up with a flower. Refer to the project photo as necessary and to the "Stencil Color Guide" at left. For detailed stenciling instructions, see "Stenciling" on page 15.

5. Allow all the paint to dry for several days; then sign and date your canvas pieces.

5. Attach the painted canvas pieces to the director's-chair frame.

WONDERFULLY WHIMSICAL
SLIPCOVERED STOOL

Finding an Ikea store on a Mother-and-Daughter shopping trip was truly a great thing for Jennifer. Not only did she find some great pieces to paint for this book, but she also solved some of her own decorating dilemmas. This stool was painted for the kids' playroom. It is fun, whimsical, and thoroughly washable.

TOOLS AND SUPPLIES

- Pastill 24" bench (Ikea #200-323-21)
- Pastill slipcover (Ikea #500-597-19)
- 4 bottles of transparent medium (DecoArt DSF1)
- Acrylic paints and stencils (see below)
- General tools and supplies (pages 7–9)

PAINTS AND STENCILS

We used the following paints and stencils to create our "Wonderfully Whimsical" project (see "Suppliers" on page 95). For a different look, substitute the colors or stencils of your choice.

DecoArt SoSoft Fabric Acrylics

- Deep Periwinkle Blue (DSS56)
- Primary Blue (DSS42)
- Christmas Red (DSS25)
- Spruce Green (DSS45)
- Hauser Light Green (DSS47)
- Antique Gold (DSS2)

Stencilled Garden Stencils

- Girly's Gone Checked (TSG222)
- Diamond Vines (TSG242L)
- Wild Animal Print (TSG128)

STENCIL COLOR GUIDE

Flowers from Girly's Gone Checked: Deep Periwinkle Blue, Primary Blue, Hauser Light Green, Spruce Green

Diamond Vines: Christmas Red, Hauser Light Green, Spruce Green

Wild Animal Print: Deep Periwinkle Blue

INSTRUCTIONS

1. Prepare the stool slipcover for painting (see "Preparing Fabric" on page 13).

2. Smooth out one section of the slipcover at a time on the cardboard painting surface, starting with the top section (see "Fabric-Painting Surface" on page 14).

3. Create a color-wash mixture for the top section, mixing eight parts transparent medium with one part Antique Gold. Using a stencil brush, scrub this color wash into the fabric, completely covering the top section of the slipcover.

4. Next, create a color-wash mixture for the end sections, mixing eight parts transparent medium with one part Deep Periwinkle Blue. Using a stencil brush, scrub this color wash into the fabric completely, covering the end sections of the slipcover.

5. Stencil the designs, referring to the project photo as necessary and to the "Stencil Color Guide" at left. For detailed stenciling instructions, see "Stenciling" on page 15.

6. After all stenciling has dried, you'll create another color wash to be applied around the flowers on the skirt area. Create a color-wash mixture using eight parts transparent medium with one part Hauser Light Green. Using a stencil brush, scrub this color wash into the fabric around all the stenciled designs.

7. Allow all the paint to dry for several days; then sign and date your stool slipcover.

8. Install the stool slipcover over the stool and enjoy for many years to come.

MOVE OVER, KITTY
OTTOMAN SLIPCOVER

Judy has an area in her home that she has created for relaxation; a place where she can put her feet up and rest for a while. This ottoman will be a great place to rest those tired feet after a long day of painting.

TOOLS AND SUPPLIES

- Ottoman (the one shown measures 22½" long x 16½" wide x 15" high)
- Green brushed cotton fabric (refer to "Cutting" on page 43 and add together the sizes of the cut pieces to determine the yardage needed)
- Lining fabric (refer to "Cutting" on page 43 and add together the sizes of the cut pieces for the skirt lining to determine the yardage needed)
- 4 black tassels, 4" long
- Black rope welting (yardage is equal to twice the perimeter of the ottoman cushion plus ¼ yard)
- Thread to match fabric
- Iron and ironing board
- Press cloth
- Sewing supplies
- Acrylic paints and stencils (see below)
- General tools and supplies (pages 7–9)

PAINTS AND STENCILS

We used the following paints and stencils to create our "Move Over, Kitty" slipcover (see "Suppliers" on page 95). For a different look, substitute the colors or stencils of your choice.

DecoArt Americana Acrylic Paints

- Wisteria (DA211)
- Violet Haze (DA197)
- Hauser Light Green (DA131)
- Plantation Pine (DA113)
- French Mauve (DA186)
- Raspberry (DA28)
- Moon Yellow (DA07)
- Marigold (DA194)
- Lamp Black (DA67)

DecoArt Easy Blend Stencil Paint

- Charcoal Grey (DEB28)

DecoArt SoSoft Fabric Acrylics

- White (DSS1)

Stencilled Garden Stencils

- Girly's Scatter Pattern (TSG123)
- Hungry Kitty (TSG720)
- Mardi Gras Banners (TSG141)
- Curvy Checks (TSG715S)

STENCIL COLOR GUIDE

Girly's Scatter Pattern: Wisteria, Violet Haze, Hauser Light Green, Plantation Pine

Hungry Kitty: Lamp Black, French Mauve, Raspberry, White, Easy Blend Charcoal Grey

Mardi Gras Banners: Wisteria, Violet Haze, French Mauve, Raspberry, Moon Yellow, Marigold, Lamp Black

Curvy Checks: Violet Haze, Lamp Black

INSTRUCTIONS

Prepare the green fabric for painting (see "Preparing Fabric" on page 13).

Cutting

Ottoman Top: Determine the cut size of the ottoman top piece by measuring the top of your ottoman cushion and adding ¾" all around (¼" for ease and ½" for seam allowances). Cut a piece of green fabric to this size.

Boxing Strips: Determine the cut size of the boxing strips by measuring the length and depth of the boxing strip on each side of the ottoman. Add ¾" to each end of the strips (¼" for ease and ½" for seam allowances) and add ½" along each of the long sides for seam allowances. Cut four boxing strips from green fabric to the determined dimensions.

Skirt Sides: Determine the cut size of the skirt pieces by measuring the length of each side of the ottoman and then measuring from the lower edge of the boxed cushion to the floor. Add 1¼" on each side (¼" for ease, ½" for seam allowances, and ½" for facings) and 1" to the bottom of the skirt pieces (½" for seam allowance and ½" for facing). Add ½" to the top for the seam allowance. Cut a skirt piece from green fabric to the determined dimensions for each side of the ottoman.

Skirt Corners: Determine the cut size of the skirt-corner pieces by measuring from the lower edge of the boxed cushion to the floor and adding 1½" (1" for two ½" seam allowances and ½" for lower facing). Cut four corner pieces from green fabric 6¼" wide by the determined length.

Skirt Lining for Sides: Determine the cut size of the skirt-lining pieces by measuring the length of each side of the ottoman and then measuring from the lower edge of the boxed cushion to the floor. Add ½" to the top of the skirt-lining pieces for seam allowances and ¼" to the sides for ease (side and bottom seam allowances are already included). Cut four skirt-lining pieces to the determined measurements.

Skirt Lining for Corners: Determine the cut size of the skirt-corner-lining pieces by measuring from the lower edge of the boxed cushion to the floor and adding ½" for the seam allowance at the top edge (seam allowance for lower edge is already included). Cut four corner-lining pieces 6¼" wide by the determined length.

STENCILING

1 Smooth out one piece of the green fabric at a time onto the cardboard painting surface (see "Fabric-Painting Surface" on page 14).

2 Stencil the designs onto the fabric pieces, creating one piece for the top, four boxing strips for the sides, and four skirt pieces. Refer to the project photo as necessary and to the "Stencil Color Guide" provided on page 43. You'll need to adjust the spacing of your stencil designs along the sides of the boxing strip and along the skirt panels if your ottoman measurements are different from this one. For detailed stenciling instructions, see "Stenciling" on page 15. The skirt-corner and skirt-lining pieces are left unpainted.

3 Allow all the paint to dry for several days; then heat-set the painted fabric (see "Heat-Setting" on page 14). Sign and date the painted fabric.

Assembling the Ottoman Slipcover

1 Stitch the boxing strips together end to end in a continuous strip, stitching them in the order needed to go around the sides of the ottoman cushion. Press the seams open.

2 Pin the rope welting to both long edges of the boxing strip. Turn the ends into the seam allowance where they meet. Stitch the welting in place, using a zipper foot.

3 Pin the continuous boxing strip to the ottoman top piece, right sides together, aligning the seam lines of the boxing strip with the corners of the top piece. Stitch just inside the previous stitching next to the welting, using a zipper foot. Clip the boxing strip into the seam allowance at the corners and clip the heading of the welting strip if necessary. Set aside.

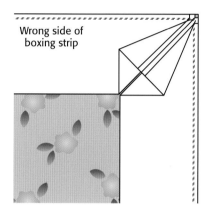

Wrong side of boxing strip

4 Stitch a skirt-corner piece to a skirt-corner lining piece, right sides together, along one short edge. Trim the seam allowance and press toward the green fabric. Fold the piece in half, right sides together, matching raw edges. Stitch ½" from each long side. Trim seam allowances, turn right side out, and press. Baste raw edges together at the upper edge. Repeat to make three additional lined corner pieces.

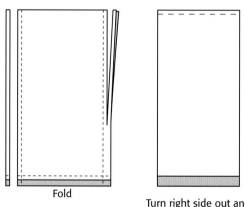

Fold

Trim seam allowances.

Turn right side out and baste along upper edge.

⑤ Pin a stenciled skirt piece to a corresponding skirt-lining piece along the lower edge, centering the lining piece along the length of the skirt piece. Stitch ½" from the raw edges. Trim the seam allowance and press toward the green fabric. Fold the piece in half, wrong sides together, aligning the raw edges at the upper edge. Baste together along the upper edge. Press ½" to the back side along both ends; then press over ½" again. Hand stitch the pressed edges in place. Repeat for the remaining three skirt pieces.

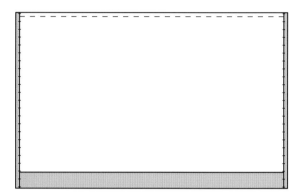

Hand stitch along the sides of the skirt.

⑥ Align adjacent sides of the skirt pieces and center a skirt-corner piece under the join. Pin; then baste in place. Repeat with the remaining skirt pieces and corner pieces to make one continuous skirt strip.

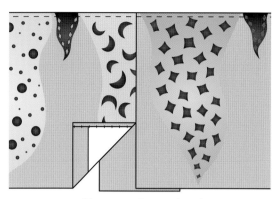

Center skirt-corner piece under adjoining skirt pieces and baste in place.

⑦ Pin the skirt right sides together to the raw edge of the boxing strip, aligning the splits in the skirt with the seam lines of the boxing strip. Stitch next to the welting, just inside the previous stitching, using a zipper foot. Press the seam toward the boxing strip. Turn the slipcover right side out.

⑧ Hand stitch the tassels to the corners of the slipcover along the bottom row of rope cording.

⑨ Place the slipcover over your ottoman.

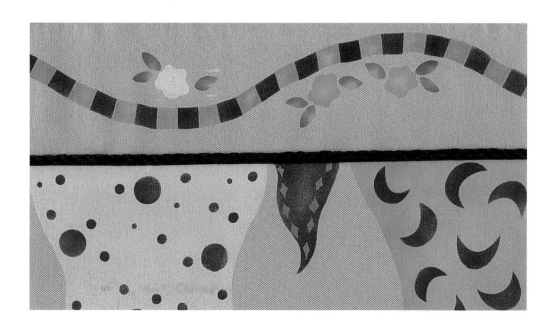

REJOICING
COVERED CORNICE

Jennifer has been updating and remodeling her home since moving in four years ago. Her latest big project was a complete remodeling of the kitchen. With the remodeling portion of the job completed, it was time to add the finishing touches, which included this wonderful cornice.

TOOLS AND SUPPLIES

Trim yardages are determined by the size of the cornice. Refer to the project photo for placement.

- ¼"-thick plywood (see step 1 on page 47 to determine amount)
- Natural denim fabric (see step 3 on page 48 to determine yardage needed)
- Lining fabric (see steps 8 and 9 on page 48 and 49 to determine yardage needed)
- Batting (see step 6 on page 48 to determine yardage needed)
- Black bullion fringe, 3" long
- Black 3-ply cording, ⅜" diameter
- 3 bottles of transparent medium (DecoArt DSF1)

- Angle irons and screws for installing cornice
- Fabric marking pen
- Fabric scissors
- Hot glue gun and glue sticks
- Staple gun and staples
- Table saw
- Wood glue
- Wood screws and screwdriver
- Acrylic paints and stencils (see below)
- General tools and supplies (pages 7–9)

PAINTS AND STENCILS

We used the following paints and stencils to create our "Rejoicing" cornice (see "Suppliers" on page 95). For a different look, substitute the colors or stencils of your choice.

DecoArt SoSoft Fabric Acrylics
- White (DSS1)
- Deep Periwinkle Blue (DSS56)
- Lamp Black (DSS24)

DecoArt Americana Acrylic Paints
- Reindeer Moss Green (DA187)
- Plantation Pine (DA113)

Stencilled Garden Stencils
- Tori's Tulips (TSG163)
- Joy Hope Peace Faith Love (TSG877)

INSTRUCTIONS

1 Measure your window to determine the width, length, and depth of the cornice. Take into account any other window treatments, such as sheers mounted on a rod or outside-mounted blinds, that the cornice will need to fit over. To make the cornice, you'll need one front, two sides and one top, all cut from ¼"-thick plywood. The front of the cornice shown here features a shaped lower edge. To create smooth curves, trace around a drinking glass to shape the inside and outside curves along the lower edge. The assembly diagram below lists the dimensions of the pieces used for this cornice. Use it as a guide to calculate the dimensions for your cornice pieces, factoring in the wood thickness, and cut the pieces with a table saw. Assemble the cornice box as shown, securing the pieces together with wood screws and wood glue. (Jennifer recruited a woodworker to build the cornice for her.)

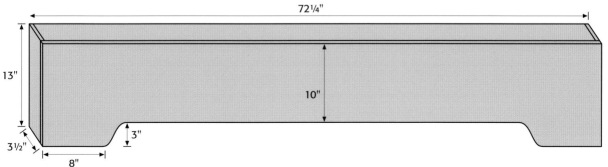

Cornice Assembly

② Prepare the natural denim fabric for painting (see "Preparing Fabric" on page 13).

③ Cut a piece of fabric large enough to cover the sides, front, and top of the cornice, allowing about 4" more on all sides to wrap the fabric to the inside of the cornice. Smooth out one section of the fabric at a time onto the cardboard painting surface (see "Fabric-Painting Surface" on page 14).

④ Apply a color wash over the entire piece of the fabric. Mix together eight parts transparent medium with one part each of the white and Deep Periwinkle Blue fabric paint. Using a stencil brush, scrub this color wash into the fabric completely, covering all fabric. Allow to dry completely.

⑤ Stencil the designs, referring to the project photo as necessary and to the "Stencil Color Guide" provided on page 47. For detailed stenciling instructions, see "Stenciling" on page 15. Allow to dry completely.

⑥ Follow the instructions below to cover the cornice box with your stenciled fabric, or do as Jennifer did and take the cornice, batting, lining, trims, and stenciled fabric to an upholsterer. To cover the cornice yourself, first cut a piece of batting to the measurement of the outside of the cornice with the height equal to the longest measurement of the front piece. Adhere the batting to the front and sides of the cornice with spray adhesive, trimming away any excess along the shaped lower edge. Smooth the stenciled fabric over the front and around the sides of the cornice box and staple to the inside of the box at the sides. Fold fabric to the inside of the cornice along the

lower edge and staple in place, folding in excess fabric at the corners; clip along the inside curves and make tucks in the fabric along the outside curves of the shaped lower edge as necessary for a smooth fit. Fold the fabric over the top of the cornice at the sides first and staple in place. Then fold the fabric at the front over the top to the inside, creating a mitered fold in the fabric at the corners on the top of the cornice (similar to wrapping a package). Staple as necessary along the top mitered fold. Pull the fabric snug to the inside and staple in place. Continue stapling the fabric to the cornice all around as necessary for a smooth fit. Trim the fabric close to the staples.

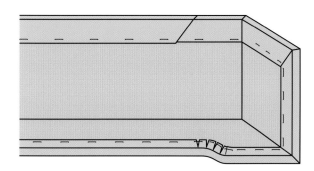

⑦ Place the cornice front on the lining fabric and trace around the cornice with a fabric marking pen. To the ends, add the depth of the cornice and then cut out the fabric ½" outside the marked lines.

⑧ Turn the cornice wrong side up and center the lining over the inside front and sides. At the upper edge, staple the lining to the top of the cornice along the seam allowance. Staple the fabric to the inside of the cornice along the corners. At the bottom and side edges, turn under the excess fabric and staple the lining in place along the inside edges of the cornice; clip the lining within the seam allowance around the shaped lower edge if necessary.

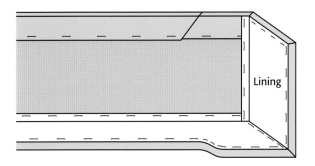

9 Cut another piece of lining equal to the dimensions of the inside top of the cornice, allowing for ½" seam allowances all around. Turn under the seam allowances and staple in place along the inside top of the cornice.

10 Using a hot glue gun, attach the fringe to the lower edge of the cornice box. Cut the three-ply cording in half. Tape two ends to a work surface and twist the cords together. Tape the ends together at the opposite end. Using a hot glue gun, glue the cording along the upper edge of the cornice.

11 Sign and date your completed cornice. Use angle irons to hang the cornice above the window. Position the angle irons at the ends of the cornice and about 3½' apart across the cornice. Attach the angle irons to wall studs wherever possible, and if securing to drywall or plaster, use hardware appropriate for supporting the weight of the cornice.

VERDALEE SWIRLS
PULL-DOWN WINDOW SHADE

This stenciled window shade was a necessary replacement for an old window shade that was hanging in Jennifer's house when she bought it. Jennifer loved the idea of using a pull-down shade because it allows full light or privacy when wanted. Also, this shade provided her with yet another great surface to paint on—and the kitchen needed a little whimsy.

TOOLS AND SUPPLIES

Trim yardages are determined by the size of the shade. Refer to the project photo for placement.

- White linen shade with scalloped edge
- Black 3-ply cording, ⅜" diameter
- Black bullion fringe, 3" long
- Chip brush

- Extender
- Faux glazing medium
- Hot glue gun and glue sticks
- Terry-cloth rag
- Acrylic paints and stencils (see page 51)
- General tools and supplies (pages 7–9)

PAINTS AND STENCILS

We used the following paints and stencils to create our "Verdalee Swirls" shade (see "Suppliers" on page 95). For a different look, substitute the colors or stencils of your choice.

DecoArt Americana Acrylic Paints

- Dried Basil Green (DA198)

Stencilled Garden Stencils

- Double Checks (TSG713-3)
- Verdalee Swirls (TSG525)

INSTRUCTIONS

1. Measure the window area to determine the width and length of the window shade. Either purchase a ready-made shade or order one custom made to your specifications through the Stencilled Garden (see "Sources" on page 95).

2. Remove the wooden stick from the pocket at the bottom of the shade. Create a negative glazed background on the entire shade (see "Negative Glazed Finishes" on page 18). Start by mixing four parts faux glazing medium with one part Dried Basil Green paint. Use a chip brush to apply the glaze mixture to your project. To create the broken colored effect and to eliminate brushstrokes, gather up a terry-cloth rag and "pounce" it over the glazed surface, removing some of the glaze and creating a soft texture. Allow the finish to dry thoroughly.

3. Using the Double Checks stencil, stencil the shade completely, creating an allover repeated pattern. Stencil, using the Dried Basil Green mixed with extender to create a more transparent coloration. Stencil down to the fold of the pocket for the wood stick and allow it to dry. Then fold up the pocket, realign the stencil, and stencil the underside of the pocket and the scalloped bottom of the shade.

4. Using the Verdalee Swirls stencils, stencil the three separate designs randomly all over the checks, creating a layered look. Space the stencils a uniform distance apart without overlapping them. Stencil, using the Dried Basil Green paint mixed with just a little extender to produce a tone-on-tone painted look. Refer to the project photo as necessary. For detailed stenciling instructions, see "Stenciling" on page 15.

5. Allow all the paint to dry. Reinsert the wooden stick into the pocket at the bottom of the shade; sign and date your pull-down shade.

6. Cut the three-ply cording in half. Tape two ends to a work surface and twist the cords together. Tape the ends together at the opposite end. Using a hot glue gun and glue sticks, secure the cording to the bottom of the shade along the pocket for the wood stick, referring to the project photo for placement. Wrap the ends to the wrong side and secure with glue. Secure the bullion fringe along the bottom of the shade with hot glue, wrapping the ends to the back side.

7. Install the shade in your window and enjoy your painted handiwork.

BELLA FLOURISH SWIRLS
DRAPERY PANELS

After faux finishing all the walls in her family room, Jennifer still felt as though something was missing. These great drapery panels added the splash of color the room needed. She stenciled them with a tone-on-tone look, creating a very soft and subtle pattern for the room.

Tools and Supplies

- Two tab-style drapery panels
- Acrylic paints and stencils (see below)
- General tools and supplies (pages 7–9)

Paints and Stencils

We used the following paints and stencils to create our "Bella Flourish Swirls" drapery (see "Suppliers" on page 95). For a different look, substitute the colors or stencils of your choice.

DecoArt SoSoft Fabric Acrylics

- Alizarin Crimson (DSS55)

Stencilled Garden Stencils

- Bella Flourish Border (TSG530L)

Instructions

1. Prepare the drapery panels for painting (see "Preparing Fabric" on page 13).

2. Smooth out one section of the drapery panel at a time onto the cardboard painting surface (see "Fabric-Painting Surface" on page 14).

3. Stencil the border design vertically on the drapery panel, using the Alizarin Crimson paint, to create a stripe pattern. Create as many vertical stripes across the drapery panel as will fit, leaving an even amount of space between each stenciled stripe. Refer to the project photo as necessary. For detailed stenciling instructions, see "Stenciling" on page 15.

4. Allow all the paint to dry; then sign and date your drapery panels.

5. Hang the drapery panels on a decorative rod.

GONE '60s
WINDOW VALANCE

A great way to soften any window is to add a valance, and this one makes a fun statement. With the retro look very popular right now, this makes a great window treatment for a young girl's room, a playroom, or even a kitchen.

TOOLS AND SUPPLIES

Trim yardage is determined by the width of the valance. Refer to the project photo for placement.

- 1 tab-top valance in white or off-white (the one shown above is a white stripe)
- Decorative purple fringe

- Iron and ironing board
- Press cloth
- Transparent medium (DecoArt DSF1)
- Acrylic paints and stencils (see page 55)
- General tools and supplies (pages 7–9)

PAINTS AND STENCILS

We used the following paints and stencils to create our "Gone '60s" valance (see "Suppliers" on page 95). For a different look, substitute the colors or stencils of your choice.

DecoArt Americana Acrylic Paints

- Hauser Light Green (DA131)
- Gooseberry Pink (DA27)
- Violet Haze (DA197)
- Wisteria (DA211)
- Lamp Black (DA67)

Stencilled Garden Stencils

- Gone '60s (TSG816)

INSTRUCTIONS

1 Prepare the valance for painting (see "Preparing Fabric" on page 13).

2 Smooth out one section of the valance at a time onto the cardboard painting surface (see "Fabric-Painting Surface" on page 14).

3 Stencil the designs, referring to the project photo as necessary. For detailed stenciling instructions, see "Stenciling" on page 15.

4 To create the color-washed background, mix eight parts transparent medium with one part Hauser Light Green. Using a stencil brush, scrub this color wash into the fabric, going around all the stenciling.

5 Allow the paint to dry; then heat-set the paint (see "Heat-Setting" on page 14). Sign and date your painted valance.

6 Install the valance on a decorative rod.

Floorcloths have been one of Jennifer's favorite things to paint for many years. Most people still can't believe that they are really made for walking on, but they are a wonderful way to create a custom "rug" for any room. This fun piece was created for the foyer of her home—a whimsical way to greet guests.

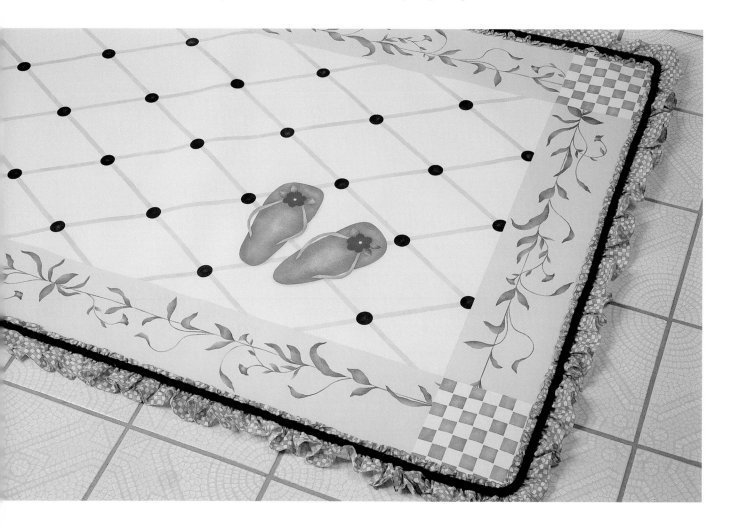

TOOLS AND SUPPLIES

- Floorcloth canvas (the one shown measures 33½" x 58")
- 1 yard of blue checked fabric for ruffle
- 5¼ yards of black 3-ply rope cording, ⅜" diameter
- Thread to match checked fabric
- Acrylic polymer varnish
- Bowling-alley paste wax (Home Trends; see "Suppliers" on page 95)
- Foam roller
- Hot glue gun
- Glue sticks
- Pencil
- 2 rags
- Rubber padding or rug gripper

- Sewing supplies
- Acrylic paints and stencils (see below)
- General tools and supplies (pages 7–9)

PAINTS AND STENCILS

We used the following paints and stencils to create our "Gracefully Stepping In" floorcloth (see "Suppliers" on page 95). For a different look, substitute the colors or stencils of your choice.

DecoArt Americana Acrylic Paints

- Country Blue (DA41)
- Soft Lilac (DA237)
- Wisteria (DA211)
- Violet Haze (DA197)
- Hauser Light Green (DA131)
- Plantation Pine (DA113)
- Payne's Grey (DA167)
- Napa Red (DA165)
- Lamp Black (DA67)
- French Vanilla (DA184)
- Light Buttermilk (DA164)
- Santa Red (DA170)

Stencilled Garden Stencils

- Graceful Vine (TSG221)
- Connect the Dots (TSG246L)
- Bizzy's Beach Sandals (TSG831)
- ¾" Checkerboards (TSG706)

STENCIL COLOR GUIDE

Graceful Vine: Soft Lilac, Country Blue, Payne's Grey, Hauser Light Green, Plantation Pine

Connect the Dots: Soft Lilac, Lamp Black

Bizzy's Beach Sandals: Wisteria, Violet Haze, Santa Red, Napa Red, French Vanilla, Hauser Light Green, Plantation Pine

Checkerboards: Country Blue

INSTRUCTIONS

1. Determine the desired size of the floorcloth canvas. Using a ruler and pencil, mark the canvas with straight lines and cut the piece out with scissors.

2. Apply a Light Buttermilk base coat over the entire floorcloth with a foam roller. Apply as many coats as necessary to achieve smooth, opaque coverage. Allow to dry.

3. Next, using removable painter's tape, measure and mark a 6" border along each side of the floorcloth and mark off 6" corner squares as shown. Burnish the edges of the tape well to help prevent seepage.

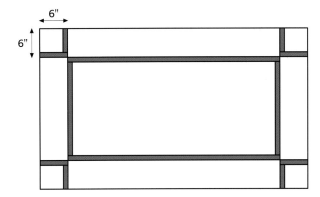

4. Paint the four 6"-wide border sections with French Vanilla, applying as many coats as necessary to achieve smooth, opaque coverage. Allow to dry and remove the tape.

5. Stencil the designs, referring to the project photo on page 56 and the "Stencil Color Guide" at left. To layer the sandals over the "Connect the Dots" pattern, you'll do what is referred to as "whiting out" (see "To white out" on page 17). First, position the sandal stencil over the painted background and secure it with tape. Use a stencil brush to apply gesso through the stencil. Leave the

stencil in place and allow the gesso to dry. (If you like, you may use a blow dryer to speed up the drying process.) Then stencil your design with the paints indicated in the "Stencil Color Guide," stenciling directly over the white gesso coat. Never remove the stencil overlay until you've applied all the colors necessary.

6 Sign and date your floorcloth. Allow the paint to dry for several days. Apply at least three to four coats of acrylic polymer varnish to protect your work. This type of varnish will dry more flexible than most, which is an important factor for floorcloths.

7 To protect the varnish finish and to provide a surface that's easy to clean, apply one to two layers of bowling-alley paste wax. Apply with a rag, and then use another clean rag to buff the finish.

8 Instead of creating a "hemmed" edge on the rug, Jennifer added a ruffled fabric trim. To make the ruffle, cut a piece of fabric 3½" wide by twice the perimeter of the rug; piece widths of fabric together to achieve the correct length. Sew a narrow hem on one edge of the strip. Press under 1" on the remaining side and stitch two rows of gathering threads ⅝" and ¾" from the fold. Pull up the gathering threads, spacing the gathers evenly, and tape the ruffle every few inches along the outer edge of the floorcloth, with the gathering threads placed about ¼" from the edges of the floorcloth to fit the ruffle to the floorcloth. Remove the ruffle and

stitch between the rows of gathering threads to secure the ruffles in place. Tape the ruffle back into position on the floorcloth and glue in place with the hot glue gun. Position the line of glue under the rows of gathering threads and remove the pieces of tape as you come to them. Then attach the cording over the gathering stitches with the hot glue gun. The ruffled edge will provide additional weight around the edge of the floorcloth and help it lie flat.

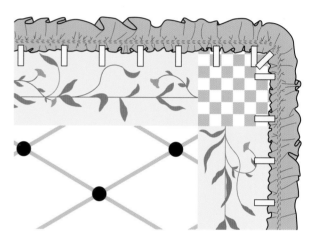

Gather ruffle to fit around the outer edge of the floorcloth and tape in place.

9 Cut the rubber pad or rug gripper slightly smaller than the rug, not including the ruffle. Place the rubber pad or rug gripper on the floor and cover it with the floorcloth. Make sure that the floor surface is clear of any particles before putting your rug in place, because any debris under the floorcloth creates a bump in the cloth, which could cause more wear on that area.

IT'S ALL ABOUT CHERRIES
LAMP AND SHADE

By now, if you have read any of the other books Jennifer and Judy have written, you know that Jennifer has a love for cherries. This lamp had been sitting around her studio for many more years than she would like to admit, but apparently it had been just sitting there waiting for the perfect project. After she added the stenciled red drapery panels (page 52) to her family room, she thought another red piece would be great to create balance—finally the inspiration she needed to complete this lamp.

TOOLS AND SUPPLIES

Trim yardages are determined by the size of the shade. Refer to the project photo for placement.

- Lamp base (prewired)
- Lamp shade
- 5 wooden ball knobs, 1½" diameter
- Black braid trim, ½" wide
- Black tasseled fringe trim, 2" wide
- Embossing tool
- E6000 industrial-strength adhesive
- Acrylic paints and stencils (see below)
- General tools and supplies (pages 7–9)

PAINTS AND STENCILS

We used the following paints and stencils to create our "It's All about Cherries" project (see "Suppliers" on page 95). For a different look, substitute the colors or stencils of your choice.

DecoArt Americana Acrylic Paints

- Tomato Red (DA169)
- Wisteria (DA211)
- Violet Haze (DA197)
- Evergreen (DA82)
- Hauser Light Green (DA131)
- Lamp Black (DA67)
- Light Buttermilk (DA164)
- Buttermilk (DA03)

DecoArt SoSoft Fabric Acrylics

- Alizarin Crimson (DSS55)
- Christmas Red (DSS25)
- Hauser Light Green (DSS47)
- Hauser Dark Green (DSS46)
- Lamp Black (DSS24)

Stencilled Garden Stencils

- La De Da Flowers (TSG171)
- Fresh Cherries (TSG223)
- Ashley's Tea Party (TSG183)
- Checkerboards (TSG706)

STENCIL COLOR GUIDE

Dots from La De Da Flowers

Fabric Paints: Lamp Black

Fresh Cherries

Fabric Paints: Alizarin Crimson, Christmas Red, Hauser Light Green, Hauser Dark Green

Acrylic Paints: Wisteria, Violet Haze, Hauser Light Green, Evergreen

Flowers from Ashley's Tea Party

Acrylic Paints: Light Buttermilk, Buttermilk, Hauser Light Green, Evergreen

Checkerboards

Acrylic Paints: Lamp Black

INSTRUCTIONS

1. Prepare the lamp base and wooden ball knobs for painting (see "Preparing an Old Wood Surface" on page 13).

2. Paint the lamp base and one of the wooden ball knobs with Tomato Red acrylic paint. Paint the other four wooden ball knobs with Lamp Black acrylic paint. Apply as many coats as necessary to achieve smooth, opaque coverage (see "Base-Coat Painting" on page 15).

3. Stencil the designs on the lamp base using the acrylic paints that are listed. Refer to the project photo as necessary and to the "Stencil Color Guide" at left for placement. For detailed stenciling instructions, see "Stenciling" on page 15.

4. Use an embossing tool to apply Violet Haze La De Da Dots to the flower centers and Lamp Black La De Da Dots randomly around the flowers and on the red wooden ball knob. Apply Light Buttermilk La De Da Dots on the black wooden ball knobs (see "La De Da Dots" on page 18).

5. Sign and date your lamp base. Allow the paint to dry for several days. Apply at least two to three coats of varnish to all wooden parts to protect your work (see "Final Touches" on page 19).

6. Use E6000 adhesive to attach the knobs to the bottom of the lamp base. Attach the large red knob to the top of the lamp over the existing finial screw.

7. Stencil the lamp shade with the designs using the fabric paints listed. Jennifer found that it helped to use her nonstenciling hand to support the underside of the shade while stenciling. Refer to the project photo and to the "Stencil Color Guide" for placement.

8. Allow the paint to dry for several days; then sign and date your project. Embellish the shade by attaching the braid trim along the top edge and the fringe trim along the bottom edge using a hot glue gun and glue sticks.

OH LA LA!
DECORATIVE PILLOW COVERS

Any room can always use a few more pillows, and these pillows are a wonderful addition to Judy's family room.

With so many trim and fringe options available, it was hard not to go over the top with embellishments.

TOOLS AND SUPPLIES

- One 16" envelope pillow cover (BagWorks #3116)
- Two 16" pillow covers (BagWorks #3016)
- Three 16" pillow forms
- 2 yards of black fringe trim
- ¾ yard of cranberry fringe trim
- 2 yards of pink rope cording
- 4 burgundy tassels
- 1 decorative raspberry-colored satin flower, 6" diameter
- 1 berry-colored button, ⅞" diameter
- Sewing supplies
- Thread to match fabrics and trims
- Fabric marking pen
- Iron and ironing board
- Press cloth
- Transparent graph ruler
- Acrylic paints and stencils (see page 62)
- General tools and supplies (pages 7–9)

PAINTS AND STENCILS

We used the following paints and stencils to create our collection of "Oh La La!" projects (see "Suppliers" on page 95). For a different look, substitute the colors or stencils of your choice.

DecoArt Americana Acrylic Paints

- Cranberry Wine (DA112)
- Lamp Black (DA67)
- Hauser Light Green (DA131)
- Flesh Tone (DA78)
- Santa Red (DA170)
- Napa Red (DA165)
- Plantation Pine (DA113)

DecoArt Easy Blend Stencil Paint

- Charcoal Grey (DEB28)

Stencilled Garden Stencils

- Wild Animal Print (TSG128)
- Oh La La (TSG256)
- Ms Jubee (TSG741)
- Rosie Posies (TSG167)
- Zebra Shoe (TSG248)

STENCIL COLOR GUIDE

Wild Animal Print: Lamp Black

Oh La La: Lamp Black

Ms Jubee: Cranberry Wine, Flesh Tone, Lamp Black, Hauser Light Green, Santa Red, Napa Red

Rosie Posies: Cranberry Wine, Hauser Light Green, Plantation Pine, Lamp Black

Zebra Shoe: Cranberry Wine, Lamp Black, Easy Blend Charcoal Grey

OH LA LA! PILLOW

1. Prepare the pillow cover for painting (see "Preparing Fabric" on page 13).

2. Smooth out the pillow cover onto the cardboard painting surface (see "Fabric-Painting Surface" on page 14).

3. Using your transparent ruler and fabric pen, mark off approximately 2" for the outside border and tape off with removable painter's tape. Burnish the edge of the tape to prevent seepage.

4. Create a color wash by mixing eight parts transparent medium with one part Cranberry Wine paint. Using a stencil brush, scrub this wash into the fabric on the outside of the taped edge; remove tape when finished.

5. Stencil the designs. Refer to the photo as necessary and to the "Stencil Color Guide" at left for placement. For detailed stenciling instructions, see "Stenciling" on page 15.

6. Sign and date your pillow. Allow the paint to dry; then heat-set the paint (see "Heat-Setting" on page 14). Hand stitch the black fringe trim to the outer edges. Insert the pillow form into the cover.

ANIMAL PRINT PILLOW

1. Prepare the pillow cover for painting. (See "Preparing Fabric" on page 13.)

2. Smooth out the pillow cover onto the cardboard painting surface. (See "Fabric-Painting Surface" on page 14.)

3. Create a color wash by mixing eight parts transparent medium with one part Cranberry Wine paint. Using a stencil brush, scrub this wash into the fabric, covering both sides of the pillow completely. Allow to dry.

4. Stencil the designs. Refer to the project photos as necessary and to the "Stencil Color Guide" on page 62 for placement. For detailed stenciling instructions, see "Stenciling" on page 15.

5. Sign and date your pillow. Allow the paint to dry; then heat-set the paint (see "Heat-Setting" on page 14).

6. Hand stitch the pink rope cording around the outer edges of the pillow and attach the tassels to the corners of the pillow. Hand stitch the rose to the top right corner of the pillow as shown.

ZEBRA SHOE PILLOW

1. Prepare the pillow cover for painting. (See "Preparing Fabric" on page 13.)

2. Smooth out the pillow cover onto the cardboard painting surface. (See "Fabric-Painting Surface" on page 14.)

3. Create a color wash by mixing eight parts transparent medium with one part Cranberry Wine paint. Using a stencil brush, scrub the wash into the fabric on the top flap section and the entire back side of the pillow.

4. Stencil the designs. Refer to the project photo as necessary and to the "Stencil Color Guide" on page 62 for placement. For detailed stenciling instructions, see "Stenciling" on page 15.

5. Sign and date your pillow. Allow the paint to dry; then heat-set the paint (see "Heat-Setting" on page 14).

6. Stitch a button to the pillow under the buttonhole. Hand stitch the cranberry fringe trim around the outer edge of the envelope flap. Button the flap in place.

LADYBUG, LADYBUG
SHEETS AND PILLOWCASE

Jennifer says she has been blessed with a wonderful sister-in-law, Trisha, who has several children (seven, to be exact). Jennifer has enjoyed painting projects for Trisha and her family over the years and helping to decorate. This set of sheets was created to match another project that was made for the girls' room. However, this is just the beginning. There are two more beds that still need matching sheets!

TOOLS AND SUPPLIES

- 1 set of yellow twin sheets and pillowcase
- Acrylic paints and stencils (see below)
- General tools and supplies (pages 7–9)

PAINTS AND STENCILS

We used the following paints and stencils to create our "Ladybug, Ladybug" linens (see "Suppliers" on page 95). For a different look, substitute the colors or stencils of your choice.

DecoArt SoSoft Fabric Acrylics

- Christmas Red (DSS25)
- Lamp Black (DSS24)
- Cadmium Yellow (DSS3)
- Antique Gold (DSS2)
- Deep Periwinkle Blue (DSS56)
- Primary Blue (DSS42)
- Hauser Light Green (DSS47)
- Hauser Dark Green (DSS46)

Stencilled Garden Stencils

- Missy Miss Lady Bug (TSG735)
- Wild Posies (TSG190)
- Lazy Dazy Flower (TSG733)
- Swirlie Flower (TSG731)
- Puffy Flower (TSG734)
- Squiggles and Swirls (TSG705)

STENCIL COLOR GUIDE

Missy Miss Lady Bug: Christmas Red, Lamp Black

Wild Posies: Deep Periwinkle Blue, Primary Blue, Hauser Light Green, Hauser Dark Green

Lazy Dazy Flower, Swirlie Flower, and Puffy Flower: Deep Periwinkle Blue, Primary Blue, Cadmium Yellow, Antique Gold

Squiggles and Swirls: Lamp Black

INSTRUCTIONS

1. Prepare the sheets and pillowcase for painting (see "Preparing Fabric" on page 13).

2. Smooth out a section of the sheets and pillowcase onto the cardboard painting surface (see "Fabric-Painting Surface" on page 14).

3. Stencil the designs, referring to the project photo as necessary and to the "Stencil Color Guide" above. For detailed stenciling instructions, see "Stenciling" on page 15.

4. Allow the paint to dry for several days. Sign and date your project and then make the bed.

ROSIE POSIES ALL AROUND
DECORATIVE BEDROOM NETTING

Jennifer and her daughter, Ashley, were shopping at Ikea when Ashley saw this bedroom netting and fell in love

with the idea of adding it to her room. Jennifer thought it would add a finishing touch to the room and decided to

personalize it with some painting.

TOOLS AND SUPPLIES

- Bedroom netting (Ikea)
- 16 small purple flower buttons, ½" diameter
- Hand-sewing needle
- Iron and ironing board
- Press cloth
- Acrylic paints and stencils (see below)
- General tools and supplies (pages 7–9)

PAINTS AND STENCILS

We used the following paints and stencils to create our "Rosie Posies All Around" project (see "Suppliers" on page 95). For a different look, substitute the colors or stencils of your choice.

DecoArt Americana Acrylic Paints

- Wisteria (DA211)
- Violet Haze (DA197)
- Hauser Light Green (DA131)
- Plantation Pine (DA113)

Stencilled Garden Stencils

- Rosie Posies Flower (TSG200L)

INSTRUCTIONS

1. Iron the netting with a warm iron to remove any wrinkles.

2. Smooth out one section at a time onto the cardboard painting surface (see "Fabric-Painting Surface" on page 14).

3. Stencil the designs randomly over the netting, referring to the project photo as necessary. For detailed stenciling instructions, see "Stenciling" on page 15.

4. Sew the decorative buttons along the edges of the netting's front opening, spacing them about 11" apart.

5. Sign and date your project. Allow the paint to dry; then heat-set the paint (see "Heat-Setting" on page 14). Then hang the netting over the head of the bed from a decorative hook in the ceiling.

ALL AMERICAN
TABLECLOTH

Jennifer and her family love to entertain friends and relatives as often as possible. With a large extended family like hers, Jennifer needs many tablecloths. This is one that she painted with the Fourth of July in mind. Creating different themed tablecloths for all the holidays is lots of fun, and this tablecloth is an especially fun and easy project.

TOOLS AND SUPPLIES

- White tablecloth, 52" square
- Transparent medium (DecoArt DSF1)
- Acrylic paints and stencils (at right)
- General tools and supplies (pages 7–9)

PAINTS AND STENCILS

We used the following paints and stencils to create our "All American" tablecloth (see "Suppliers" on page 95). For a different look, substitute the colors or stencils of your choice.

DecoArt SoSoft Fabric Acrylics

- Primary Blue (DSS42)
- Christmas Red (DSS25)
- Hauser Light Green (DSS47)
- Spruce Green (DSS45)
- Lamp Black (DSS24)

Stencilled Garden Stencils

- Every Little Star (TSG832)
- American Pie (TSG238)
- 1" Checkerboards (TSG706)

STENCIL COLOR GUIDE

Every Little Star: Primary Blue

American Pie: Christmas Red, Hauser Light Green, Spruce Green, Lamp Black

Checkerboards: Christmas Red

INSTRUCTIONS

1. Prepare your tablecloth for painting (see "Preparing Fabric" on page 13).

2. Smooth out one section of the tablecloth at a time onto the cardboard painting surface (see "Fabric-Painting Surface" on page 14).

3. Tape off the hemmed edge of the tablecloth to create a border using removable painter's tape. The hemmed edge on this tablecloth measures 1½". Burnish the edges of the tape to help prevent paint seepage.

4. Create a color wash by mixing four parts transparent medium with one part Primary Blue paint. Using a stencil brush, scrub the wash into the fabric on the outside edge of the tablecloth to create the border; remove tape when finished.

5. Stencil the designs, referring to the project photo as necessary and to the "Stencil Color Guide" at left. For detailed stenciling instructions, see "Stenciling" on page 15.

6. Allow the paint to dry for several days. Sign and date your tablecloth and get ready to dine.

STRAWBERRIES ON THE VINE
PLACE MATS AND NAPKINS

When Judy found this set of place mats and napkins, she just fell in love with the style and knew it would be perfect for her daughter. Staying with the theme she had already created, Judy layered two stencil designs for a little whimsy and sophistication.

Tools and Supplies

- Set of 4 place mats and napkins with crocheted edging
- Iron and ironing board
- Press cloth
- Acrylic paints and stencils (see below)
- General tools and supplies (pages 7–9)

Paints and Stencils

We used the following paints and stencils to create our "Strawberries on the Vine" table linens (see "Suppliers" on page 95). For a different look, substitute the colors or stencils of your choice.

DecoArt Americana Acrylic Paints

- Soft Lilac (DA237)
- Country Blue (DA41)
- Tomato Red (DA169)
- Santa Red (DA170)
- Hauser Light Green (DA131)
- Plantation Pine (DA113)

Stencilled Garden Stencils

- Harliquen (TSG232)
- Strawberry Vine (TSG412)

Stencil Color Guide

Harliquen: Soft Lilac, Country Blue

Strawberry Vine: Tomato Red, Santa Red, Hauser Light Green, Plantation Pine

Instructions

1. Prepare the fabric for painting (see "Preparing Fabric" on page 13).

2. Smooth out a place mat and napkin onto the cardboard painting surface (see "Fabric-Painting Surface" on page 14).

3. First, stencil the Harliquen design as a complete allover pattern, then stencil the Strawberry pattern over the top to create a layered look. Refer to the project photo as necessary and to the "Stencil Color Guide" above. For detailed stenciling instructions, see "Stenciling" on page 15.

4. Sign and date your project. Allow the paint to dry; then heat-set the paint (see "Heat-Setting" on page 14).

WHAT'S COOKING?
APRON AND POT HOLDERS

Rather than remodel her kitchen, Judy chose to give it a face-lift with lots of paint and stencils. With such a bright and cheerful new kitchen, she needed to create an apron and pot holders to go with the newly painted room. The apron and pot holders work equally well for grilling outdoors.

TOOLS AND SUPPLIES

- Yellow apron
- 2 yellow pot holders
- Iron and ironing board
- Press cloth
- Acrylic paints and stencils (see below)
- General tools and supplies (pages 7–9)

PAINTS AND STENCILS

We used the following paints and stencils to create our "What's Cooking?" project (see "Suppliers" on page 95). For a different look, substitute the colors or stencils of your choice.

DecoArt Americana Acrylic Paints

- Santa Red (DA170)
- Napa Red (DA165)
- Violet Haze (DA197)
- Wisteria (DA211)
- Tangelo Orange (DA196)
- Marigold (DA194)

DecoArt SoSoft Fabric Acrylics

- Lamp Black (DSS24)
- Deep Periwinkle Blue (DSS56)
- Hauser Dark Green (DSS46)
- Avocado Green (DSS19)
- Light Soft Sage (DSS49)
- Hauser Light Green (DSS47)

Stencilled Garden Stencils

- Penny's Poultry Gone Wild (TSG142)
- ¾" and 1" Checkerboards (TSG706)
- Wild Posies (TSG190)
- Chickie Eggs (TSG727)
- Complete Alphabet (TSG810-L)

STENCIL COLOR GUIDE

Penny's Poultry Gone Wild

Acrylic Paints: Santa Red, Napa Red, Violet Haze, Wisteria, Tangelo Orange, Marigold

Fabric Paints: Lamp Black, Deep Periwinkle Blue, Hauser Dark Green, Avocado Green, Light Soft Sage

Checkerboards

Fabric Paints: Lamp Black

Wild Posies

Acrylic Paints: Santa Red, Napa Red

Fabric Paints: Hauser Light Green, Hauser Dark Green

Chickie Eggs

Acrylic Paints: Santa Red, Napa Red, Violet Haze, Marigold

Fabric Paints: Deep Periwinkle Blue, Lamp Black, Light Soft Sage, Avocado Green, Hauser Light Green, Hauser Dark Green

Complete Alphabet

Fabric Paints: Lamp Black

INSTRUCTIONS

1. Prepare the apron and pot holders for painting (see "Preparing Fabric" on page 13).

2. Smooth out the apron and pot holders onto the cardboard painting surface (see "Fabric-Painting Surface" on page 14).

3. Stencil the designs, referring to the project photo as necessary and to the "Stencil Color Guide" at left. For detailed stenciling instructions, see "Stenciling" on page 15.

4. Sign and date your project. Allow the paint to dry; then heat-set the paint (see "Heat-Setting" on page 14).

APPLE DELICIOUS
DISH TOWELS

Both Jennifer and Judy enjoy painting projects for their family and friends. Judy thought the apple theme of these dish towels would be perfect for her daughter, Corri. Judy has painted many things for Corri's fruit-themed kitchen. What a wonderful addition these dish towels will be!

TOOLS AND SUPPLIES

- Set of 4 white dish towels (these came with woven side borders)
- Iron and ironing board
- Press cloth
- Acrylic paints and stencils (see below)
- General tools and supplies (pages 7–9)

PAINTS AND STENCILS

We used the following paints and stencils to create our "Apple Delicious" towels (see "Suppliers" on page 95). For a different look, substitute the colors or stencils of your choice.

DecoArt Americana Acrylic Paints

- Burnt Umber (DA64)
- Hauser Light Green (DA131)
- Plantation Pine (DA113)
- Taffy Cream (DA05)
- Tomato Red (DA169)
- Moon Yellow (DA07)
- Marigold (DA194)
- Lamp Black (DA67)

Stencilled Garden Stencils

- Apple Border (TSG235)
- Trudy's Apple Pie (TSG194)
- Summertime (TSG176)

STENCIL COLOR GUIDE

Apple Border: Burnt Umber, Hauser Light Green, Plantation Pine, Taffy Cream, Tomato Red

Leaf pattern from Trudy's Apple Pie: Hauser Light Green, Plantation Pine

Ladybugs from Summertime: Tomato Red, Moon Yellow, Marigold, Lamp Black

INSTRUCTIONS

1. Prepare the dish towels for painting (see "Preparing Fabric" on page 13).
2. Smooth out one of the dish towels onto the cardboard painting surface (see "Fabric-Painting Surface" on page 14).
3. Stencil the designs, referring to the project photo as necessary and to the "Stencil Color Guide" above. For detailed stenciling instructions, see "Stenciling" on page 15.
4. Sign and date your project. Allow the paint to dry; then heat-set the paint (see "Heat-Setting" on page 14).

ALL BUGGY
MARKET UMBRELLA

Baseball is a big part of Jennifer's family life, with a husband that coaches at college level and Little League, and a son that also plays. She and Ashley find themselves at many games throughout the year. This year they will be "styling" with their new umbrella at all the games—and they'll stay a little cooler too. This large, yet portable umbrella can provide shade wherever you need it. It works great for a trip to the beach or lake!

TOOLS AND SUPPLIES

- Cotton umbrella
- Transparent medium (DecoArt DSF1)
- Acrylic paints and stencils (see below)
- General tools and supplies (pages 7–9)

PAINTS AND STENCILS

We used the following paints and stencils to create our "All Buggy" umbrella (see "Suppliers" on page 95). For a different look, substitute the colors or stencils of your choice.

DecoArt SoSoft Fabric Acrylics

- Blue Shimmering Pearls (DSP8)
- Light Teal Shimmering Pearls (DSP16)
- Teal Shimmering Pearls (DSP11)
- Bright Blue Metallics (DSM11)
- Lamp Black (DSS24)
- Christmas Red (DSS25)
- Lavender (DSS12)
- Antique Gold (DSS2)

- Primary Yellow (DSS37)
- Antique Mum (DSS54)
- Deep Periwinkle Blue (DSS56)
- Primary Blue (DSS42)
- Hauser Light Green (DSS47)

Stencilled Garden Stencils
- Checked Butterfly (TSG736)
- Mama Lady Bug (TSG724)
- Dragonfly (TSG836)
- Bumble Bee (TSG729)
- Aloha (TSG164)

STENCIL COLOR GUIDE

Checked Butterfly: Lavender, Lamp Black

Mama Lady Bug: Christmas Red, Lamp Black

Dragonfly: Blue, Light Teal, and Teal Shimmering Pearls; Bright Blue Metallics; Lamp Black

Bumble Bee: Primary Yellow, Antique Gold, Lamp Black, Antique Mum

Aloha: Deep Periwinkle Blue, Primary Blue, Antique Gold

INSTRUCTIONS

1. Remove the fabric portion of the umbrella from the frame and prepare your umbrella fabric for painting (see "Preparing Fabric" on page 13). If the fabric portion of your umbrella can't be removed for prewashing, you can still paint it, but be sure to allow the paint to cure for 21 days before exposing the umbrella to rain or water.

2. Smooth out one section of the umbrella at a time onto the cardboard painting surface (see "Fabric-Painting Surface" on page 14). If the fabric portion of your umbrella can't be removed from the frame for painting, you'll need to use one hand to provide support on the back of the canvas while stenciling.

3. Stencil the designs, referring to the project photo as necessary and to the "Stencil Color Guide" at left. For detailed stenciling instructions, see "Stenciling" on page 15.

4. Create a color-wash background by mixing eight parts transparent medium with one part Hauser Light Green. Using a stencil brush, scrub the wash into the fabric, going around all the stenciled designs.

5. Allow the paint to dry for several days. Sign and date your project and stay cool.

SWINGING CHERRIES
HAMMOCK

Judy wanted to create a special place to hang out with her three grandchildren: Josh, Samantha, and Presli. What an incredible place to be—snuggled up with "Jubee" in the great hammock. And no matter how old you get, you can always snuggle up with your grandma.

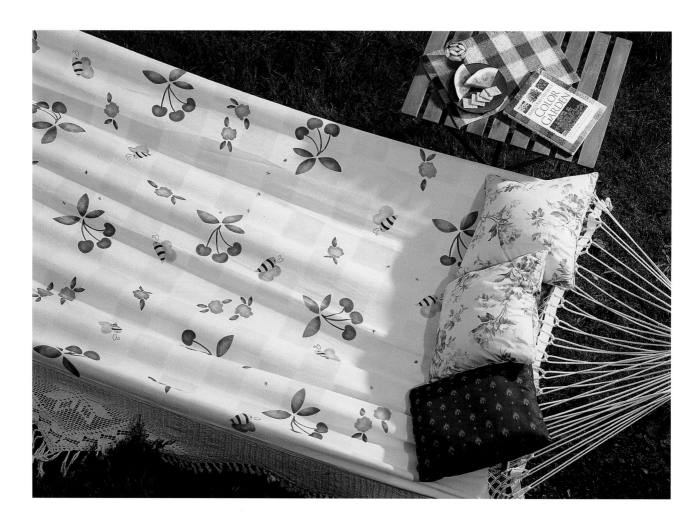

TOOLS AND SUPPLIES

- Hammock (Hangouts; see "Suppliers" on page 95)
- Iron and ironing board
- Press cloth
- Acrylic paints and stencils (at right)
- General tools and supplies (pages 7–9)

PAINTS AND STENCILS

We used the following paints and stencils to create our "Swinging Cherries" hammock (see "Suppliers" on page 95). For a different look, substitute the colors or stencils of your choice.

DecoArt Americana Acrylic Paints

- French Vanilla (DA184)
- Santa Red (DA170)
- Napa Red (DA165)
- Hauser Light Green (DA131)
- Plantation Pine (DA113)
- Burnt Umber (DA64)
- Moon Yellow (DA07)
- Antique Gold (DA09)
- Lamp Black (DA67)
- Soft Lilac (DA237)
- Country Blue (DA41)

DecoArt Easy Blend Stencil Paint

- Charcoal Grey (DEB28)

Stencilled Garden Stencils

- Double Checks (TSG713-5)
- Cherry Pickin (TSG709L)
- Bumble Bee (TSG729)
- Girly's Flower Border (TSG122)
- Whimsy Critters (TSG828)
- Elizabeth's Garden (TSG173)

STENCIL COLOR GUIDE

Double Checks: French Vanilla

Cherry Pickin: Santa Red, Napa Red, Hauser Light Green, Plantation Pine, Burnt Umber

Bumble Bee:

Acrylic Paints: Moon Yellow, Antique Gold, Lamp Black

Easy Blend Stencil Paint: Charcoal Grey

Girly's Flower Border: Soft Lilac, Country Blue, Hauser Light Green, Plantation Pine

Ladybug from Whimsy Critters: Santa Red, Napa Red, Lamp Black

Ants from Elizabeth's Garden: Lamp Black

INSTRUCTIONS

1. Prepare the hammock for painting (see "Preparing Fabric" on page 13).

2. Smooth out one section of the hammock at a time onto the cardboard painting surface (see "Fabric-Painting Surface" on page 14).

3. Stencil the designs, referring to the project photo as necessary and to the "Stencil Color Guide" above. Stencil ladybugs at each end of the hammock and stencil ants randomly in groups across the entire hammock. For detailed stenciling instructions, see "Stenciling" on page 15.

4. Sign and date your project. Allow the paint to dry; then heat-set the paint (see "Heat-Setting" on page 14).

RAINING ANIMAL PRINTS
UMBRELLA

Judy has a true love for animal prints, and she believes everything you paint can use a little animal print. Now, Judy can even stay dry in style—that's animal style. People will definitely take notice when they see this painted umbrella. They will all want to know where they can get one too.

TOOLS AND SUPPLIES

- Cotton umbrella
- Acrylic paints and stencils (see below)
- General tools and supplies (pages 7–9)

PAINTS AND STENCILS

We used the following paints and stencils to create our "Raining Animal Prints" umbrella (see "Suppliers" on page 95). For a different look, substitute the colors or stencils of your choice.

DecoArt SoSoft Fabric Acrylics

- Light Soft Sage (DSS49)
- Avocado Green (DSS19)
- Deep Periwinkle Blue (DSS56)
- Lamp Black (DSS24)

Stencilled Garden Stencils

- Jubee's Cow Spots (TSG231)
- Wild Animal Print (TSG128)
- Giraffe Print (TSG230)
- Animal Print (TSG127)

STENCIL COLOR GUIDE

Jubee's Cow Spots
> Panel 1: Light Soft Sage, Avocado Green
> Panel 6: Deep Periwinkle Blue, Lamp Black

Wild Animal Print
> Panel 3: Light Soft Sage, Avocado Green
> Panel 8: Deep Periwinkle Blue, Lamp Black

Giraffe Print
> Panel 5: Light Soft Sage, Avocado Green
> Panel 2: Deep Periwinkle Blue, Lamp Black

Animal Print
> Panel 4: Deep Periwinkle Blue, Lamp Black
> Panel 7: Light Soft Sage, Avocado Green

INSTRUCTIONS

1. Remove the fabric portion of the umbrella from the frame and prepare your umbrella fabric for painting (see "Preparing Fabric" on page 13). If the fabric portion of your umbrella can't be removed for prewashing, you can still paint it, but be sure to allow the paint to cure for 21 days before exposing the umbrella to rain or water.

2. Smooth out one section of the umbrella at a time onto the cardboard painting surface (see "Fabric-Painting Surface" on page 14). If the fabric portion of your umbrella can't be removed from the frame for painting, you'll need to use one hand to provide support on the back of the canvas while stenciling.

3. Stencil the designs, referring to the project photo as necessary and to the "Stencil Color Guide" above. For detailed stenciling instructions, see "Stenciling" on page 15.

4. Allow the paint to dry for several days. Sign and date your project. Now you'll be protected from the rain in style.

JUBEE'S BAG
TOTE BAG

While traveling and attending shows, Judy often takes projects with her to work on. This fabulous bag, which Judy created, will hold all her stuff in true style. It's sure to get lots of attention from other show attendees.

TOOLS AND SUPPLIES

- Tote bag (Bag Works #2633; see "Suppliers" on page 95)
- 4 wooden ball knobs, 2¼" diameter
- ¼ yard of ball fringe in periwinkle
- Iron-on letters
- ¼"-thick plywood
- Embossing tool
- Hot glue gun and glue sticks
- Iron and ironing board
- Kraft paper
- Pencil
- Press cloth
- Saw
- Wood screws and screwdriver
- Acrylic paints and stencils (see below)
- General tools and supplies (pages 7–9)

PAINTS AND STENCILS

We used the following paints and stencils to create our "Jubee's Bag" project (see "Suppliers" on page 95). For a different look, substitute the colors or stencils of your choice.

DecoArt Americana Acrylic Paints
- Wisteria (DA211)
- Violet Haze (DA197)
- Lamp Black (DA67)
- Hauser Light Green (DA131)
- Plantation Pine (DA113)
- Marigold (DA194)
- Olive Green (DA56)

DecoArt Easy Blend Stencil Paint
- Charcoal Grey (DEB28)

Stencilled Garden Stencils
- La De Da Flowers (TSG171)
- Tori's Tulips (TSG163)
- Curvy Checks (TSG715S)
- Honey Pot (TSG193)
- Squiggles and Dots (TSG178)
- ¾" Checkerboards (TSG706)

STENCIL COLOR GUIDE

La De Da Flowers: Wisteria, Violet Haze

Tori's Tulips: Wisteria, Violet Haze, Hauser Light Green, Plantation Pine

Curvy Checks: Hauser Light Green, Lamp Black

Honey Pot:
- Acrylic Paints: Marigold, Lamp Black
- Easy Blend Stencil Paint: Charcoal Grey

Squiggles and Dots: Lamp Black

Checkerboards: Lamp Black

INSTRUCTIONS

1. Place the tote bag on kraft paper and trace around the bottom. Cut on the marked line to make a pattern for the bottom of the bag. Trace the pattern onto ¼"-thick plywood. Cut just inside the marked line to make a wood support to fit into the bottom of the bag.

2. Prepare the plywood and wooden ball knobs for painting (see "Preparing a New Wood Surface" on page 13).

3. Apply as many Olive Green base coats as necessary to achieve smooth, opaque coverage on the plywood base and wooden ball knobs.

4. Use an embossing tool to apply Lamp Black La De Da Dots to the wooden ball knobs (see "La De Da Dots" on page 18).

5. Allow the paint to dry for several days. Apply at least two to three coats of varnish to all wooden parts to protect your work (see "Final Touches" on page 19).

6. Prepare the tote bag for painting (see "Preparing Fabric" on page 13).

7. Smooth out a section of the tote bag the best you can onto the cardboard painting surface (see "Fabric-Painting Surface" on page 14).

8. Stencil the designs, referring to the project photo as necessary and to the "Stencil Color Guide" at left. For detailed stenciling instructions, see "Stenciling" on page 15.

9. Sign and date your project. Allow the paint to dry; then heat-set the paint (see "Heat-Setting" on page 14).

10. Place the painted plywood base in the bottom of the bag. Attach the wooden ball knobs to the bottom of the bag with screws by screwing through the wood base, through the fabric, and into the knobs.

11. Glue ball fringe to the upper edge of the center pocket and fuse iron-on lettering in place.

BEE HAPPY
BANNER

It's always nice to have something in a room that makes you smile, and this banner will bring a smile to all who visit Judy. With just stuff Judy had lying around, she created a wonderful banner to fill an empty space on a wall and to remind everyone to Bee Happy!

TOOLS AND SUPPLIES

- Banner (BagWorks #4001; see "Suppliers" on page 95)
- 1½ yards of black rope cording
- ⅝ yard of beaded fringe trim
- 1 black tassel
- 1 black tasseled chair tieback
- Wooden dowel, ¾" diameter and 19½" long
- 2 clear-glass drawer pulls with screws
- Fabric marking pen
- Hot glue gun and glue sticks
- Iron and ironing board
- Press cloth
- Transparent graph ruler
- Transparent medium (DecoArt DSF1)
- Acrylic paints and stencils (see below)
- General tools and supplies (pages 7–9)

PAINTS AND STENCILS

We used the following paints and stencils to create our "Bee Happy" banner (see "Suppliers" on page 95). For a different look, substitute the colors or stencils of your choice.

DecoArt Americana Acrylic Paints

- Summer Lilac (DA189)
- Plum (DA175)
- Hauser Light Green (DA131)
- Plantation Pine (DA113)
- Camel (DA191)
- Honey Brown (DA163)
- Marigold (DA194)
- Lamp Black (DA67)

DecoArt Easy Blend Stencil Paint

- Charcoal Grey (DEB28)

DecoArt SoSoft Fabric Acrylics

- Lamp Black (DSS24)
- White (DSS1)

Stencilled Garden Stencils

- 1" Checkerboards (TSG706)
- Folk Art Posies (TSG241)
- Buzzy Beeskep (TSG826)
- Bee Happy (TSG177)
- Complete Alphabet (TSG810)

STENCIL COLOR GUIDE

Checkerboards: Lamp Black, White

Folk Art Posies: Summer Lilac, Plum, Hauser Light Green, Plantation Pine

Buzzy Beeskep: Camel, Honey Brown, Lamp Black

Bee Happy
  Acrylic Paints: Marigold, Lamp Black
  Easy Blend Stencil Paint: Charcoal Grey

Complete Alphabet: Lamp Black

INSTRUCTIONS

1. Prepare the banner for painting (see "Preparing Fabric" on page 13).

2. Smooth out the banner onto the cardboard painting surface (see "Fabric-Painting Surface" on page 14).

3. Using your transparent graph ruler and fabric pen, measure and mark off a 1½" border with removable painter's tape. Burnish the edges of the tape to help prevent seepage.

4. To create a color wash, mix four parts transparent medium with one part Summer Lilac paint. Using a stencil brush, scrub this wash into the fabric on the outside edge of the tape, creating a painted border; remove tape when finished.

5. Stencil the designs, referring to the project photo as necessary and to the "Stencil Color Guide" at left. For detailed stenciling instructions, see "Stenciling" on page 15.

6. Sign and date your project. Allow the paint to dry; then heat-set the paint (see "Heat-Setting" on page 14).

7. Glue the beaded fringe to the back of the banner along the lower edge, trimming off any excess. Insert the black cording through the sleeve at the top of the banner. Slip the tassel onto the black cording on the left side and slide down to the banner. Determine the desired length of the black cording hanger and knot ends together. Trim the excess cording. Pull the cording through the sleeve until the knot is hidden in the sleeve.

8. Paint the wooden dowel with Lamp Black acrylic paint and allow to dry. Then insert the dowel into the sleeve at the top of the banner. Attach the drawer pulls to the ends of the wooden dowel, using screws.

9. Wrap the tasseled chair tieback around the dowel on the right side of the banner, allowing the tassels to hang at different lengths. Use the project photo as a guide for placement. Enjoy your banner and Bee Happy!

FISHIES HANGING OUT
HANGING LAUNDRY BAG

Judy and Jennifer have always found enjoyment in painting for their families and for extended members of their families. Judy's future daughter-in-law, Joanie, has a nephew, Evan, and Judy knew his room was decorated in "fishies." So, Judy went to work and created this great clothes hamper for Evan's room.

TOOLS AND SUPPLIES

- Hanging laundry bag
- Iron and ironing board
- Press cloth
- Acrylic paints and stencils (see below)
- General tools and supplies (pages 7–9)

PAINTS AND STENCILS

We used the following paints and stencils to create our "Fishies Hanging Out" laundry bag (see "Suppliers" on page 95). For a different look, substitute the colors or stencils of your choice.

DecoArt Americana Acrylic Paints

- Olive Green (DA56)
- Hauser Light Green (DA131)
- French Vanilla (DA184)
- Moon Yellow (DA07)
- Country Blue (DA41)
- Santa Red (DA170)

DecoArt SoSoft Fabric Acrylics

- Lamp Black (DSS24)
- White (DSS1)

Stencilled Garden Stencils

- Charming Fishy Fish (TSG542)
- Fishy Flowers (TSG165)

STENCIL COLOR GUIDE

Charming Fishy Fish: Olive Green, Hauser Light Green, French Vanilla, Moon Yellow, Country Blue, Santa Red, Lamp Black, White

Fishy Flowers: Moon Yellow, Country Blue, Santa Red, Lamp Black

INSTRUCTIONS

1. Prepare the laundry bag for painting (see "Preparing Fabric" on page 13).

2. Smooth out the bag onto the cardboard painting surface (see "Fabric-Painting Surface" on page 14).

3. Stencil the designs, referring to the project photo as necessary and to the "Stencil Color Guide" above. For detailed stenciling instructions, see "Stenciling" on page 15.

4. Sign and date your project. Allow the paint to dry; then heat-set the paint (see "Heat-Setting" on page 14).

WHIMSICAL WHIMSY GARDEN
SHOWER CURTAIN

Judy is decorating one of her bathrooms in a whimsical garden theme. When she went looking for a shower curtain to match the room, she came up empty-handed. With no other choice, she created exactly what she wanted. Remember: if you can't find what you want, you can always paint what you need.

TOOLS AND SUPPLIES

- Natural cotton shower curtain
- Iron and ironing board
- Press cloth
- Acrylic paints and stencils (see below)
- General tools and supplies (pages 7–9)

PAINTS AND STENCILS

We used the following paints and stencils to create our "Whimsical Whimsy Garden" project (see "Suppliers" on page 95). For a different look, substitute the colors or stencils of your choice.

DecoArt Americana Acrylic Paints

- Hauser Light Green (DA131)
- Plantation Pine (DA113)
- French Mauve (DA186)
- Raspberry (DA28)
- Violet Haze (DA197)
- Wisteria (DA211)
- Marigold (DA194)
- Summer Lilac (DA189)
- Plum (DA175)
- Moon Yellow (DA07)
- Antique Gold (DA09)
- Santa Red (DA170)
- Napa Red (DA165)
- Soft Lilac (DA237)
- Country Blue (DA41)
- Light Avocado (DA106)
- Desert Turquoise (DA44)
- Dazzling Metallics Ice Blue (DA075)
- Dazzling Metallics Green Pearl (DA122)

DecoArt Easy Blend Stencil Paint

- Charcoal Grey (DEB28)

DecoArt SoSoft Fabric Acrylics

- Lamp Black (DSS24)
- White (DSS1)
- Grey Sky (DSS28)
- Dark Chocolate (DSS25)
- Burnt Sienna (DSS41)

Stencilled Garden Stencils

- Garden Grass (TSG738)
- Tall Grass (TSG739)
- Stems and Leaves (TSG740)

- Puffy Flower (TSG734)
- Lazy Dazy Flower (TSG733)
- Petal Flower (TSG730)
- Swirlie Flower (TSG731)
- Polka-Dot Flower (TSG732)
- Missy Miss Lady Bug (TSG735)
- Mr. Attitude (TSG829)
- Mouser (TSG722)
- Whimsy Critters (TSG828)
- Whimsey Mailbox (TSG742)
- Butterfly Dance (TSG168)
- La De Da Flowers (TSG171)
- Squiggles and Dots (TSG178)
- Cherries Jubillee (TSG184)
- Elizabeth's Garden (TSG173)
- Dragonfly (TSG836)
- Mama Lady Bug (TSG724)
- Bumble Bee (TSG729)
- Lady Bug Dance (TSG169)
- Checked Butterfly (TSG736)
- Complete Alphabet (TSG810)
- Tweetie Birdhouse (TSG507)

STENCIL COLOR GUIDE

Garden Grass: Hauser Light Green, Plantation Pine

Tall Grass: Hauser Light Green, Plantation Pine

Stems and Leaves: Hauser Light Green, Plantation Pine

Puffy Flower: French Mauve, Raspberry

Lazy Dazy Flower: Violet Haze, Wisteria, Moon Yellow, Marigold

Petal Flower: Summer Lilac, Plum, Moon Yellow, Antique Gold

Swirlie Flower: Santa Red, Napa Red, Moon Yellow, Marigold, Antique Gold

Polka-Dot Flower: Soft Lilac, Country Blue, Moon Yellow, Marigold

Missy Miss Lady Bug: Santa Red, Napa Red, Lamp Black

Mr. Attitude: Light Avocado, Plantation Pine, Lamp Black, White

Mouser

    Fabric Acrylics: Grey Sky

    Easy Blend Stencil Paint: Charcoal Grey

Whimsy Critters: Moon Yellow, Marigold, Santa Red, Napa Red, Lamp Black, Hauser Light Green, Desert Turquoise, Dazzling Metallics Ice Blue, Dazzling Metallics Green Pearl

Whimsey Mailbox

    Acrylic Paints: Soft Lilac, Country Blue, Santa Red, Napa Red, Hauser Light Green, Plantation Pine, Moon Yellow, Marigold, Lamp Black

    Easy Blend Stencil Paint: Charcoal Grey

Butterfly Dance: Santa Red, Napa Red, Hauser Light Green, Plantation Pine

Dots from La De Da Flowers: Santa Red

Squiggles and Dots: Lamp Black

Cherries Jubillee: Santa Red, Napa Red, Hauser Light Green, Plantation Pine, Burnt Sienna

Ants from Elizabeth's Garden: Lamp Black

Dragonfly: Hauser Light Green, Dazzling Metallics Green Pearl, Desert Turquoise, Dazzling Metallics Ice Blue, Lamp Black

Mama Lady Bug: Santa Red, Napa Red, Lamp Black

Bumble Bee:

    Acrylic Paints: Moon Yellow, Marigold, Lamp Black

    Easy Blend Stencil Paint: Charcoal Grey

Lady Bug Dance: Santa Red, Lamp Black

Checked Butterfly: Wisteria, Violet Haze, Lamp Black

Complete Alphabet: Lamp Black

Tweetie Birdhouse: Soft Lilac, Country Blue, Lamp Black, Burnt Sienna, Dark Chocolate

INSTRUCTIONS

1. Prepare the shower curtain for painting (see "Preparing Fabric" on page 13).

2. Smooth out one section of the shower curtain at a time onto the cardboard painting surface (see "Fabric-Painting Surface" on page 14).

3. Stencil the designs, referring to the project photo as necessary and to the "Stencil Color Guide" above. For detailed stenciling instructions, see "Stenciling" on page 15.

4. Sign and date your project. Allow the paint to dry; then heat-set the paint (see "Heat-Setting" on page 14).

EVERYTHING BUT THE KITCHEN SINK
SHOE BAG

When Judy saw this shoe bag, she knew it would be a challenge. Judy will hang this great piece in her work studio.

Not only will it show how to use different stencils together, but the pockets will hold different supplies; there are 24

pockets for brushes, drawer pulls, wooden knobs, papers, trim, and so much more. What a fun piece to have!

TOOLS AND SUPPLIES

- Hanging canvas shoe bag, 19" x 64½"
- Assorted decorative trims:
  - ⅝ yard of green beaded trim, 2" wide, for lower edge of top border
  - ⅜ yard of brush fringe, 1½" wide, for upper edge of pocket 1 in row 1
  - ⅜ yard of turquoise ball fringe, 1" wide, for upper edge of pocket 2 in row 2
  - ⅜ yard of crystal beaded fringe, 1¼" wide, for upper edge of pocket 4 in row 2
  - ⅜ yard of orchid beaded fringe, 1½" wide, for upper edge of pocket 3 in row 3
  - ⅜ yard of burgundy brush fringe, 1½" wide, for upper edge of pocket 1 in row 4
  - ⅜ yard of blue beaded fringe, 1¼" wide, for upper edge of pocket 1 in row 5
  - ⅜ yard of periwinkle ball fringe, 1" wide, for upper edge of pocket 4 in row 5
  - ⅜ yard of black brush fringe, 1" wide, for upper edge of pocket 3 in row 6
- Hot glue gun and glue sticks
- Iron and ironing board
- Press cloth
- Acrylic paints and stencils (see below)
- General tools and supplies (pages 7–9)

PAINTS AND STENCILS

We used the following paints and stencils to create our "Everything but the Kitchen Sink" project (see "Suppliers" on page 95). For a different look, substitute the colors or stencils of your choice.

DecoArt Americana Acrylic Paints

- Hauser Light Green (DA131)
- Lamp Black (DA67)
- Wisteria (DA211)
- Violet Haze (DA197)
- Plantation Pine (DA113)
- Burnt Umber (DA64)
- Burnt Orange (DA16)
- Santa Red (DA170)
- Marigold (DA194)
- Admiral Blue (DA213)
- Desert Turquoise (DA44)
- Soft Lilac (DA237)
- Dazzling Metallics Green Pearl (DA122)
- Dazzling Metallics Ice Blue (DA075)
- Mauve (DA26)
- French Mauve (DA186)
- Summer Lilac (DA189)
- Plum (DA175)
- Country Blue (DA41)
- Camel (DA191)
- Honey Brown (DA163)

DecoArt Easy Blend Stencil Paint

- Charcoal Grey (DEB28)

DecoArt SoSoft Fabric Acrylics

- Whites (DD101 and DSS1)
- Black (DD115)
- Cadmium Yellow (DD102)

Stencilled Garden Stencils

- Wild Posies (TSG190)
- Folk Art Tulips (TSG240)
- Springtime (TSG182)
- Strawberry Pot (TSG197)
- Honey Pot (TSG193)
- ¼" Little Checks (TSG707)
- Butterflies (TSG701)
- Wild Grapes (TSG199)
- Let's Be a Star (TSG180)
- Dragonfly Dance (TSG166)
- Whimsy Critters (TSG828)
- Garden Grass (TSG738)
- Garden Critters (TSG140)
- Ashley's Tea Party (TSG183)
- Aloha (TSG164)
- ¾" Checkerboards (TSG706)
- Girly's Flowers (TSG175)
- Folk Art Posies (TSG241)
- Trudy's Apple Pie (TSG194)
- Dazy Garden (TSG170)
- Summertime (TSG176)
- Rosie Posies (TSG167)
- Lady Bug Dance (TSG169)
- Kitty Kat Daisy's (TSG191)
- Cherrie's Jubillee (TSG184)
- Tori's Tulips (TSG163)
- La De Da Flowers (TSG171)
- Squiggles and Dots (TSG178)
- Butterfly Dance (TSG168)

STENCIL COLOR GUIDE

Wild Posies: Lamp Black, Country Blue, Soft Lilac, Plantation Pine, Hauser Light Green, Cadmium Yellow

Folk Art Tulips: Wisteria, Violet Haze, Hauser Light Green, Plantation Pine

Springtime: Burnt Umber, Burnt Orange, Hauser Light Green, Plantation Pine

Strawberry Pot: Santa Red, Hauser Light Green, Plantation Pine

Honey Pot

Acrylic Paints: Marigold, Lamp Black, Camel, Honey Brown, Plantation Pine

Easy Blend Stencil Paint: Charcoal Grey

Little Checks: Lamp Black

Butterflies: Violet Haze, Wisteria, Lamp Black

Swirls from Wild Grapes: Lamp Black

Let's Be a Star: Marigold, Santa Red, Admiral Blue, White

Dragonfly Dance: Desert Turquoise, Lamp Black

Whimsy Critters: Dazzling Metallics Green Pearl, Dazzling Metallics Ice Blue, Lamp Black

Garden Grass: Hauser Light Green, Plantation Pine

Garden Critters: Santa Red, Lamp Black

Ashley's Tea Party: Santa Red, Violet Haze, Marigold, Admiral Blue, Mauve, both Whites, Black

Aloha: Wisteria

Checkerboards: Lamp Black

Girly's Flowers: French Mauve, Mauve, Hauser Light Green, Plantation Pine, Black

Folk Art Posies: Cadmium Yellow, Plum, Hauser Light Green, Plantation Pine

Trudy's Apple Pie: Santa Red, Hauser Light Green, Plantation Pine

Curvy Checks from Dazy Garden: Lamp Black, Santa Red

Summertime: Santa Red, Lamp Black, Hauser Light Green, Plantation Pine, Marigold

Rosie Posies: Plum, Hauser Light Green, Plantation Pine, Lamp Black

Lady Bug Dance: Santa Red, Country Blue, Lamp Black, Hauser Light Green, Plantation Pine, Cadmium Yellow

Kitty Kat Daisy's: Wisteria, Violet Haze, Lamp Black

Cherries Jubillee: Santa Red, Hauser Light Green, Plantation Pine, Burnt Umber, Black

Tori's Tulips: Wisteria, Violet Haze, Hauser Light Green, Plantation Pine

La De Da Flowers: Wisteria, Violet Haze

Lady Bug Dance: Santa Red, Lamp Black

Squiggles and Dots: Lamp Black

Butterfly Dance: Marigold, Lamp Black

INSTRUCTIONS

1. Prepare the hanging shoe bag for painting (see "Preparing Fabric" on page 13).

2. Smooth out one section of the shoe bag at a time onto the cardboard painting surface. You may want to make smaller cardboard sections to fit inside of the pockets (see "Fabric-Painting Surface" on page 14).

3. You'll be creating several different color washes for backgrounds and borders. Mix four parts transparent medium to one part acrylic paint listed to create a color wash. Using a stencil brush, scrub this wash into the fabric. For borders, measure and tape off the section to be color washed, using removable painter's tape.

Outside edges and black lines between pocket rows: Create ½"-wide borders, using a Lamp Black color wash.

Top border: Create a 2"-wide border across the top, using a Hauser Light Green color wash.

Row 1: Create a ½"-wide border along the top of the second pocket using a Plantation Pine color wash. Create a ½"-wide border along the top of the third pocket using a Santa Red color wash. Completely color wash the fourth pocket with a Violet Haze color wash.

Row 2: Create a 1½"-wide border along the top of the first pocket, using a Santa Red color wash. Completely color wash the third pocket with a Soft Lilac color wash.

Row 3: Create a ½"-wide border along the top of the first pocket, using a Wisteria color wash. Completely color wash the third pocket with a Summer Lilac color wash. Create a ½"-wide border along the top of the fourth pocket, using a Santa Red color wash.

Row 4: Completely color wash the first pocket with a Plum color wash. Create a ½"-wide border along the top of the second pocket, using a Country Blue color wash. Create a 1⅞"-wide border along the top of the third pocket, using a Hauser Light Green color wash.

Row 5: Create a ½"-wide border along the top of the second pocket, using a Lamp Black color wash.

Row 6: Create a ½"-wide border along the top of the first pocket, using a Violet Haze color wash. Completely color wash the third pocket with a Hauser Light Green color wash. Create a ½"-wide border along the top of the fourth pocket, using a Lamp Black color wash.

4. Stencil the designs, referring to the project photo as necessary and to the "Stencil Color Guide" provided on page 93. For detailed stenciling instructions, see "Stenciling" on page 15.

5. Sign and date your project. Allow the paint to dry; then heat-set the paint (see "Heat-Setting" on page 14).

6. Attach the decorative trims to the upper edges of the pockets, using a hot glue gun and glue sticks. Use the project photo as a guide for placement.

The Stencilled Garden
6029 North Palm Ave.
Fresno, CA 93704
(559) 449-1764 (phone or fax)
www.stencilledgarden.com
garden@stencilledgarden.com

Stencils, brushes, paints, faux-painting tools and supplies, AC's Acrylic Craft Paint Remover, brush cleaner/conditioner, brush scrubbers, decorative accessories, linen window shades

BagWorks, Inc.
(817) 446-8080
(800) 365-7423
www.bagworks.com

Pillow covers, floorcloths, banners, aprons, totes, place mats, pot holders, director's chair seat and back, laundry bags

DecoArt
PO Box 386
Stanford, KY 40484
(800) 367-3047
www.decoart.com

Acrylic paints, fabric paints, glazes

Dharma Trading Co.
(800) 542-5227
www.dharmatrading.com

Totes, aprons, laundry bags, umbrellas, place mats, floorcloths, dish towels, pillow covers, banners

Hangouts
1328 Pearl Street Mall
Boulder, CO 80302
(800) Hangout
(303) 442-2533
www.hangouts.com

Hammocks

Home Trends
(888) 815-0814
www.shophometrends.com

Bowling-alley paste wax

IKEA
www.ikea.com

Furniture, slipcovers

Orchards Supply and Hardware
www.osh.com

Hanging laundry bag, shoe bag

Royal and Langnickel Brush Manufacturing, Inc.
6707 Broadway Ave.
Merrillville, IN 46410
(800) 247-2211

Artist's brushes, faux brushes

ABOUT THE AUTHORS

An artist, designer, and teacher of the arts of stenciling and faux finishing, Jennifer Ferguson has been painting for the past 15 years. Through her company, The Stencilled Garden, she designs stencils and pattern packets; teaches stenciling, faux finishing, and plaster finishes; and sells all the materials and supplies for these projects and techniques. Jennifer is a regular guest on the *Carol Duvall Show*, and she has also appeared on *Aleene's Creative Living, Kitty Bartholomew: You're Home*, and *Smart Solutions* with Maty Monfort, where she shared some of her ideas and projects with viewers. When she isn't attending trade shows, traveling, teaching, or painting projects, Jennifer enjoys spending time with her family,

going to all the kids' games, watching her husband coach baseball, and doing a little creative painting on their home.

An artist, "house stripper," and dedicated recycler, Judy Skinner has been creating art for more than 20 years. Through her company, Collectiques by JuBee, she recycles old windows, doors, drawers, and any other house parts she can find, transforming them into works of art. She sells her unique creations at art shows throughout California and Nevada. When she isn't attending art shows or finding houses to strip, Judy enjoys spending time with her family and finishing projects for their home.

Jennifer and Judy met at Jennifer's shop back in 1996, and since then, they've developed a wonderful friendship. Their mutual love for the arts of recycling, painting, stenciling, and faux finishing gives them much to share. They have traveled all over the United States to attend conventions and in the process have indulged in "junking" trips, which have led them to many treasures.

Painted Fabric is the fourth book for this duo, following *Painted Chairs, Painted Whimsies*, and *Trashformations*. Jennifer and Judy both hope that you enjoy this book and that you fall in love with painting.